Gray Matter

Stuff That Got Me To Thinking

Foreword

I read lots of Christian writing daily in books, articles, devotionals. Some of it is really well done as befits reflections from saints from the past and leading thinkers stimulating us in the present. But one that hits home for me with great regularity is the weekly devotional written online for United Methodist Men by one of their leaders, Charlie Gray. Here's a man who gets what we preachers have been saying about experiencing God's great love made known to us in Jesus, and how that first love is to shape our lives. May Charlie's tribe increase, and may his writing continue to bless us for years to come.

Rev. Charles M. Smith, DD

Pastor in Residence

Duke Divinity School

Thank You

I want to say "thanks" for spending your hard earned money on the purchase of this book. I hope it provides a blessing to you and others that may visit its pages.

My scribble is intended to be received in a manner more akin to a personal conversation rather than grammatically correct and edited compositions. Unapologetically cerebral pieces of prose intended to stir reflection. My life is rich in friends and family. Growing up in the simple, rural farmland of eastern North Carolina in a close knit and loving family is my being. In that is found the inspiration for my words.

I tend to write in a fragmented style. Many times the ideas fly faster than I can process. It is obvious that I am not a professional writer but simply a disciple attempting to find my way along a path of service to Jesus Christ.

My writings originated as a weekly journal several years ago and have developed into somewhat of a personal ministry for me. The notes of affirmation I receive weekly, some of which I have shared, bless me far beyond the blessings of my words to others.

However, this book is not about me or who I am. It's about my belief that Jesus Christ can change our life regardless of who we are, where we come from or whatever baggage we might have accumulated along the way. He calls us all to service in feeding the hungry, clothing the naked, providing shelter for the homeless and seeking justice for the downtrodden. Some He calls to scribble. I can only hope these simple observations of life promote reflection for the reader while bringing praise and glory to our Lord, Jesus Christ.

At the urging of friends and family, I am humbled to publish this small collection of my scribble which I am privileged to share with you. Thanks for all the love, support and encouragement.

Charlie Gray

Gold Star Mama

I was dining recently with some friends at a popular chicken wing joint. Being the eve of Veterans Day there was a larger than normal crowd of military folks in the place. Actually a member of our group was military and struck up a conversation with an adjoining table.

He pointed out a lady at the table as a Gold Star mom. She was middle age dressed very neatly in a pressed blouse and sweater. Military people are trained that way. They take pride in their appearance. Proudly displayed on her sweater was a gold star. Eventually my curiosity got the best of me so I asked my friend the significance of the gold star. He explained this identified her as a mother who had lost a child in combat. All of a sudden, my lemon pepper wings and sweet potato fries lost their taste. As we were leaving, I made a point to shake her hand which turned into a hug. I expressed my sorrow for her loss.

She responded to me with beautiful dignity and pride in her son. She explained how military service was a tradition in their family.

She told of her son's father and grandfather's service and gave me a smile that warmed my heart when she said "he died doing what he loved."

Got me to thinking ….. Veteran's Day wasn't much on my mind until I met this lady. It's not only the servicemen and women that sacrifice in war but the family also suffers great stress, pain and sometimes loss. This lady, as well as her son, was a causality of war. God knows about sacrifice. He knows about the unselfish giving of a son so others may live. God calls each of us to special places. He called my new found friend to the Gold Star ……. she wears it well.

Priceless Pets

Pets are great. We have dogs, cats, fish and a rabbit. Yes, we probably over do it. My pet of choice is the dog. My dog of choice is "Biggie:" a seventy-four pound, twelve-inch high English bulldog. I know what you're thinking ...... the "pet resembles owner" .... well go ahead. Anyway, me and Biggie are tight.

We have that unconditional connection. This guy waits for me at the back door every evening and welcomes me home like I am the most important person in the world. If I am away for a few days, my wife declares that Biggie is very much "out of sorts" until I return.

Few weeks back I could detect my friend was not feeling well so off we went to the vet. Our vet referred us to the NCSU Vet School where Biggie underwent extensive testing. It was determined he had a heart valve condition.

This condition had no cure but could possibly be controlled with some medication. It was estimated our checkbook would take a sizable punch in the gut. Some might think it next to sinful to spend thousands on a dog. Biggie returns to NCSU again this week for further observation and testing. He will probably be on medication the rest of his life. First thing I did when my wife gave me the financial report was to thank God that I have been blessed such that I can take care of my friend. This special animal brings tremendous joy to our family and all who know him. Can I place a dollar value on that?

Got me to thinking ….. Proverbs 12:10 teaches that God regards a person's care and concern for the life of an animal as righteousness. Pets are a responsibility that we should not take lightly. God has blessed man with full dominion and authority over our pets and He pays attention to how we care for them.

In today's times, we all face economic challenges and the need to budget and manage our money is a front burner issue. Even so, I thank God for my friend. He is a dog. He is a part of the family. He loves me. The joy He brings is a gift from God and for that he deserves my best - checkbook and all.

Making It Out Alive

Before we get started let me say, I'm not much for country music. With that being said, last week while channel surfing the radio I ran across a song by Hank Williams. The title was "I'll Never Get Out Of This World Alive." I listened to about half of the song before continuing my search for some Lynyrd Skynyrd or Kool and the Gang. Sorry Hank, you couldn't hold me with the song but you captured me with the title.

Fact is, contrary to the lyrics of Mr. Williams, I do intend to leave this world alive. Jesus says that those who believe in Him have, not will have, eternal life. To receive eternal life is to join God's life, which is everlasting. When we surrender our heart to Jesus Christ, we conquer death. Our soul is transformed into an everlasting dimension. Eternal life is not something that awaits us when we draw our last worldly breath. For me and all Christians, eternal life is now.

Got me to thinking ….. In John 2:24, we hear of a revolutionary promise that God has made - a promise that we can live forever. God makes that promise of eternal life for those who put their faith in Jesus Christ.

This message is for a dying world; "come those who are thirsty and weary, take the water of life freely." It is through grace, truly amazing grace, that this eternal life is offered to an undeserving, sinful people.

When our Lord calls us home, our earthly body as we know it, will be disposed of and our soul will become an active participant in His kingdom in heaven. But the thought that we leave this world dead is hogwash. This concept has no value among Christians except maybe to inspire a country music song.

Released in 1952, I'll Never Get Out Of This World Alive was the last hit by Williams. An eerie side note is the song was released just months before Williams died at age 29. While I'm not a fan of his music, I hope Hank was wrong - hope he made it out alive.

My Son ...... The Alien

WARNING ! I have an alien living under my roof. If you take the back stairs up to the second floor and take a left down the hall, his bedroom is the first on the right. He also may be spotted in the upstairs media room or roaming our yard filling his bird feeders. He is my son, his name is Joseph.

The first alien sighting was in middle school. After being assigned the task of writing a composition on "What Keeps Me Off Drugs," Joseph chose as his theme "Jesus." He wrote how his faith in Jesus gave him the strength to say no to drugs. His teacher gave him a zero on the assignment. Mind you Joseph is a straight A student. Even after his mom and I met with his principal, Joseph received a B for the year in that class because of the zero.

The second alien sighting occurred when given again another assignment of writing a paper on the "Most Influential Man in American History." Joseph chose Jesus. He was told Jesus as his topic was unacceptable. It seems the subject of his paper must have lived after 1776. I guess some folks are unaware that Jesus is alive today. He chose Billy Graham as his substitute.

Got me to thinking ..... when we become followers of Jesus, we become aliens of the world. We are no longer politically correct, no longer normal based on standards set forth by the world. Our mindset, our values, our way becomes so different from that of the world - we are paranormal.

Third Day front man Mac Powell pens these lyrics in the song Alien. " I am just like an alien - a stranger in a strange land." He further pleads "Father defend my cause."

I am proud of my son the alien. His mom and I encourage him to be courageous. He spends his summer vacation in Africa and prowls our church halls on Sunday asking the other kids to turn off their cell phones. He is secure enough in his faith not to be discouraged, shy or ashamed.

To be honest, the alien sightings bother me far more than they bother him. He takes it all in stride. When I look at myself and then look at him, I am overwhelmed with the blessing I have in him from Jesus.

Andre

A man came in my office last week and had to duck when he entered thru the doorway. He said he was 6'9" but he appeared taller - he was a giant. God makes us in all shapes and sizes. The tallest man I know barely reaches my shoulder. His worldly height has been reduced by a wheelchair.

I remember the day I met him. He was handsome with a neatly trimmed beard and very distinguished grayish hair. It was not until he spoke that I recognized his true beauty. He is a lawyer, accountant and holds a MBA. He is kind, thoughtful, graceful and direct about his relationship with Jesus. I love him - he is my brother in Christ. He carries my heart.

He moved from a fast paced law practice and a passion for black belt karate competition to the stillness of quadriplegia in one split second. His deep faith, absence of anger and presence of peace demonstrate a dimension of his relationship with God forged only through intense suffering and grief.

Got me to thinking ….. my friend has not given up on or is angry at God because something awful happened to him. Instead he has intentionally chosen a deeper level of faith and level of understanding of God's presence alongside. I ask God everyday to use me as He sees fit. Knowing my friend makes me realize that's one heck of a gamble.

My friend is seated deep enough in his faith to realize and appreciate that God is using him - it just happens to be three feet from the ground. My dear brother is courageously playing the cards he has been dealt.

I cherish this man as a friend. I am hard to hold - he grounds me. When I complain about my minor aches and pains, I think of him and realize I can walk and write my name. Trusting in Jesus has been easier for me by knowing this mountain of a man.

On that tragic day of his accident - God had a plan - a seed was planted. I and many people I know and love are reaping the fruits of that harvest. There are blessings in bad things happening to good people. There are angels in our presence. I know one, his name is Andre.

My Hero

I had a person come into my life some 54 years ago or should I say I came into their life. It was a great relationship from the very beginning. This person watched over me, provided for and took care of me. Throughout the early years of our relationship this person nourished me in body and the ways of life.

As time passed, I began to feel myself being influenced by this person. Skills and lessons were being taught. Work ethic was being instilled. The simple way of life was celebrated and an appreciation for what you had was being emphasized. As I became a teenager, sometimes a period hard on relationships, our bond became even stronger. Commitments on both sides sometimes separated us but we always came back around to center. While there were disagreements in method, we shared a commitment to common goals.

Many times I disappointed this person; however there were conversations and adjustment sessions that always left me stronger. This person was there in my accomplishments and failures, companion in laughter and tears. There beside me through the automobile accidents, the first job, the birth of my sons, the death of family and friends. Through the good and the bad, the ups and the downs, for better or worse, the relationship was firm. The commitment and the love were truly unconditional.

Later in life when I became comfortable and confident in my place, this person continued to encourage and offer advice in subtle ways. This person was outwardly proud of me. Life was good and we both enjoyed the fruits of our maturing relationship. Then came some health challenges and loss for this person. Through the amazing power of God's grace this person's life was transformed.

Not until over forty years into our relationship did Jesus enter into the mix. The substance of our final chapter is when my friend began to encourage me to follow Jesus. In a soft, non threatening way they began to share with me their love for Christ and how they were praying that I would re- prioritize some things in my life.

The person in this relationship was my dad. I recently heard that men no longer have heroes. Well, my dad was my hero. He passed on Saturday. I will miss him but I am overwhelmed with joy that he had prepared himself to meet Jesus. He offered me many things but none more precious than his witness for Christ. This relationship will never be replaced. I have no regrets. My dad finished well. He left things in a good order.

Time

I spent some time this week sending notes to folks with numbers attached to their name. John Doe #0998745. Athletes have numbers. We know Michael Jordan as number 23, Dale Earnhardt as number 3. In some instances, the number is more recognizable than the person. Well not in this case. The numbers associated with my friends this week were North Carolina Department of Correction numbers. These numbers you need to make it through life without.

I have been involved with a prison ministry for several years working with inmates in their reentry process. For many the outside is more challenging than the inside. Where do they go, where do they live, where do they work? This is a critical time and depending on what happens usually determines if they make it on the outside or if they reenter prison. Over 700,000 inmates are released each year. Well over half will return to prison within three years.

I have a file cabinet full of letters from inmates. Some letters are testimonies of rehabilitation and rebirth while others are filled with excuses and hateful blame. The overwhelming theme that flows throughout these correspondences is the concept of time. Many letters begin with "I will be released soon" only to find in the following paragraph their release date is five years down the calendar. Time is elusive and mysterious. Time is plastic in the 64 square feet world of a cell.

You think more often about time when time is all you have. Time for the inmate is everything and nothing. While we on the outside use time as a measure to sequence events, compare intervals and quantify change - there is no need of such for those whose lives are absent of any elements other than a bed, sink and toilet. Ironically, you will never see a prison cell without a calendar pinned to the wall.

Jesus knew about time. He knew from the beginning how little of it He possessed. He knew with each passing day what awaited Him in the end. Time was not on His side. Jesus wasted no time. He was quick to surround Himself with a group similar to the kinds of folk He was trying to reach. He was quick to teach, educate and delegate within His inner circle. In doing so, He also taught us not to worry about time. Much was accomplished in the three short years of His ministry.

How much time do you have?

Dad's Tractor

Sold my dad's tractor last week. He recently passed after several years in a care facility stricken with Alzheimer's. Most of his assets had been sold to facilitate his expenses but I had held on to one of his tractors, a 1950 Farmall Cub. He used this tractor for over thirty years to cultivate the large vegetable garden he tended before he became ill.

Unlike me, he had a green thumb and enjoyed sharing the bounty of his garden with friends and family. He loved that tractor. Truth is for me, hanging on to that tractor was hanging on to a part of him.

Someone asked what my dad would have thought about me selling his tractor. There is no doubt in my mind that he would understand. I know that because we were connected. We shared our lives with each other on more than a superficial level. We talked about things that were important. He told me stories - I knew his history. Full disclosure is important in authentic relationships.

Got me to thinking ….. talking with those we love is HUGE. Wes Yoder writes in his book Bond Of Brothers: "Uncover what a person is not talking about and you may discover what they care about the most."

I think that is so unfortunate. When we talk, we sometimes find silly avenues to express serious concerns. Men joke about sitting on the front porch cleaning their shotguns as they await their daughter's first date, but the thought behind the joke is dead serious. It is crucial that we cultivate environments for conversation where pain, failure and regret can be revealed free of judgment.

The conversations with my dad were gifts that invited me into his presence. Little did I know or appreciate at the time, but the glimpses of himself revealed in our relationship inspire me now and will for a lifetime. He showed me his limp and I feel my own. No regrets about selling the tractor, I know he would have approved. We talked about that a long time ago.

Wheels That Wobble

I shop a lot. Now wait a minute ladies ...... don't be envious. It is not the fun type of shopping you might enjoy. I am in Wal-Mart a couple of times per week buying supplies for work. We have a new super Wal-Mart just down the street from my office. If Wal-Mart doesn't have it - you don't need it.

The thing I dislike most about shopping is the wobbly, squeaky, bent and twisted wheels on the shopping carts. They drive me crazy. Even the carts at this new Wal-Mart are already worn and torn. Last week I was moaning and groaning while shopping with a wobbly wheel cart. Relieved to be checked out and headed for the car it all became clear.

There was a Wal-Mart employee collecting the stray carts in the parking lot and he was not being kind. I have never seen this level of disregard in my life. He was pushing carts into each other, ramming and slamming them around with absolutely no concern for their well being. There were broken carts pushed to the side and left alone and abandoned. There were carts overturned and lying on their side. There were carts in the middle of the road just waiting to be run over by a car. There just seemed to be zero concern for how the carts were being handled. No wonder their wheels wobble.

Got me to thinking ..... people are a lot like shopping carts. We are beaten, battered, pushed to the side, overloaded and left out in the cold. No wonder our wheels wobble. Solomon asked for wisdom but also received the gift of an understanding heart. Before we judge those whose wheels appear to wobble, let's first attempt to understand where they may be in their life.

Unlike the shopping carts, as children of God, we can realize His awesome glory and grace as a result of our suffering and brokenness. The pain of the world that surrounds us is real and cannot be denied. The good news is that Jesus assures us of an eternity where pain and suffering are a thing of our worldly past. A place where everything rolls with divine precision. A place of calmness and order. A place where wheels don't wobble.

Merry Christmas

December 25th, party time. The Christmas shopper on average spends $570.00 on gifts and $170.00 on the Christmas meal. I need to share these averages with my wife. It seems we always exceed that just a bit. Christmas sales account for over 20% of the total annual retail sales. One billion Christmas cards will be mailed each year. This is quite a "top shelf" birthday party for Jesus. Question: why do WE get all the stuff on HIS birthday? We have turned Christmas into a demanding, hectic time of year. More people have heart attacks on December 26th than any other day of the year.

The historic record of the birth of Christ can be found in Matthew 1:18-25 and Luke 2:1-20. What a story. It made no sense in "worldly" terms. Here we have a young, virgin woman giving birth to a child. There are a couple of accounts in the Matthew and Luke passages but regardless of the exact details, what we do know is God invaded history by taking on the form of a man.

The ancient church did not celebrate his birth. It was celebrated only by his mother, her husband, and a handful of shepherds. This new born king had barely left the manager before King Herod was after His head. As a favorite author of mine writes: "The shadow of the cross is already falling across His face."

Got me to thinking ….. about taking a real look at the nativity. Remove your Rudolph red nose colored glasses, smell the foul air, see the cold, shivering animals. Look at the players, all cast in roles of divine appointment. Yes a King is born, born to die so that all who believe in Him might live.

Sending cards, buying gifts, being with our family and eating until we are stuffed is great. We celebrate the birth of Jesus but even more let's rejoice in the life He lived, the death He died, and the accomplishment of His resurrection.

While we remember His birthday on December 25th, let our celebration and the remembrance of His death and His resurrection be lived out 365 days a year. Let's not look for a baby in a manger. He's not there. The baby grew up and changed our world for an eternity.

Get Off Your Donkey

QUESTION: What is the state of our faith without service? ANSWER: dead. Can dead faith save us? If our brother is naked and hungry, do we simply say "I wish you well, have a great day?" If we do nothing about his needs what good are we? Is faith without service simply intellectual assent - just agreement with a certain set of Christian teachings or belonging to this social club we call "church?"

I suggest true faith transforms our service as well as our hearts. Faith that is alive manifests itself - it moves us from passive sympathy or pity to active service. True faith agitates something within our souls that compels us to action. It's one thing to look at someone with pity; it's another to feel so stirred within your heart that you just have to do something.

Jesus came to this earth to make disciples. In the final days of His earthly ministry, Jesus was very clear with his disciples. Service was the verb in His plan and expectations. Not only did He emphasize their devotion to the apostles' teachings but also to give to anyone as they had need.

Got me to thinking ..... am I just a "professional Christian" going through the motions? Being versed in scripture, attending church, serving on committees, is all that stuff enough? No, walking in the steps of Jesus requires a little dirt and grime under the fingernails .... hitting the thumb with a hammer, some cuts and blisters on the hands. It involves going to strange places doing things that challenge our comfort level. Our call to service is very much about being inconvenienced.

Jesus never intended for faith and service to exist separately. His calling for our lives is fulfilled only when our hands and feet join our heart in complete service to Him and our neighbors.

My brothers, what is the gain if anyone says he has faith, but he does not have works? Is the faith able to save him?

James 2:14

See You Soon Dad

This world is surely a broken place. Given our human condition - the basic craving for blue sky, Camelot and the such - we cannot surely love it until we taste that brokenness. We can never embrace the blessing of connection until we encounter the sting of separation.

Throughout my life, I have been empathetic towards those caring for an aging parent or family member. I always communicated concern but lacked the "in your face" realization that only comes with traveling that road yourself. Taking the cruise differs from reading the brochure.

For several years I was separated from my earthly father by the demon of Alzheimer's disease. Being witness to a loved one's loss of memory and physical control is a one-two punch of immeasurable sadness thrown deep to the gut. There comes no more defining moment for a son than when he has to feed his father and wipe his runny nose. This is the same father that once fed him. The once lively face of dad is now blank and the arms once strong are now thin and trembling. This is the side of fatherhood Hallmark doesn't print on Father's Day cards. There's nothing warm and fuzzy about hanging out with your father in a nursing home. The once noisy, quick exchange conversation typical with him for years is gone. That silence is deafening, it shatters your eardrums. The father who made a habit of flattering you with his pride no longer knows your name. This state of separation is a very bad place to be.

My father and I were best friends. The separation I have from him is painful. Got me to thinking ….. the relationship I have with my heavenly father ensures that one day I will be reunited with the man I call dad.

I urge you to embrace the present. For a man there is nothing more important than your role as a son, as a father, as a man. Be prepared, the time afforded us in these roles is precious and short. It is my prayer that you will have no regrets.

Gift Of Prayer

I was riding in the car with my mother in law last week en route to one of the 824,673 events my son is involved in (that's a good thing) for the holidays. The two of us were in the front seat. I always have the honor of being the driver when we travel with the in-laws (that's also a good thing). She looks over at me and asks: "what do you want for Christmas?"

Now you have to understand my mother in law is especially generous around Christmas. Anything I asked for, within reason, I probably would get. Now the same question had already been asked a few days before by my wife so I had some time to think about it. Truth be known I need nothing material. I and my family have been richly blessed. I have a job and good health. Based on my having thought about the question, I responded that I wanted "nothing" for Christmas.

Got me to thinking ….. about my answer. Truth is, I need plenty from my mother in law this Christmas. While my material coffers may be overflowing, I am in great need of her prayers that I will be a better husband to her daughter. I need her faith that I will be a proper Christian role model for her grandson. I need her hope that I can continue to provide for our family. I need her support as the leader and head of my household.

We may think we have everything. The reality of that false sense of security is just a routine physical checkup gone bad or a tangle with a wreck less driver away. Our world can be turned upside down in a split second. When that happens, it is wise for our lives not to be fully vested in a material portfolio.

This year for the friend or family member who has it all ..... give them your prayers, your hope, your support and your love. These truly are the gifts that will keep on giving !!!!!!

Repeat Offender / Repeat Forgiver

I spent Friday inside a high level security prison. I know what you are thinking - but my attire was not orange. I was there to speak to over 300 inmates and spend some personal time with them in conversation. While I have been involved in this ministry for several years, I am never fully prepared for my encounter with this population.

These guys spend 23 hours a day in an area smaller than your SUV. There is no telephone, private toilet, no dog to chase the stick. The food is bad. Temptation, drugs, violence and intimidation is constant.

Some are here because of a split second bad decision, a $50 heist that went awry or a joy ride in someone else's car. Some are here because they are truly evil. Some look like the kid next door, well groomed and neat in appearance. Some display the worn & torn look of years on the street, permanently scarred by knives, drugs and tattoos. A vast majority have been here before ….. they are repeat offenders.

Even though I feel very much out of my element, I have never questioned why I continue to accept the invitation. As a Christian, I am uniquely equipped to stand in the gap. I have not been dealt with according to my sins having experienced the mercy of God's grace. I received this mercy not because I am reformed but because I cannot reform myself.

Got me to thinking …. I too am a repeat offender. I continue to commit sins against others and God. It is in my nature. My hope is the relationship I have with a patient God who guides me back to the right path with an undeserved love and compassion.

Each trip I make inside the walls of a prison results in more questions for me than answers. These men have murdered, raped, robbed and violated innocent victims. The message I know and carry through security check points and metal detectors is that God's capacity to love exceeds our capacity to violate one another and our desire for vengeance. I'll be back.

There Is A Santa

It's the season when that deep, mysterious question of the ages raises its head .... is there a Santa Claus? Now you may know him as Saint Nicholas, Kris Kringle, or simply Santa. Anyway, this guy delivers toys and candy to all the good boys and girls and coal and sticks to the naughty children each year on Christmas Eve. This guy even has reindeers that fly.

As a child, I remember when Kendrick, the bully in my neighborhood, first informed me that the Santa thing was all a hoax. Heck, he was the only kid I knew that could chew Red Man chewing tobacco without getting sick - to be sure he was a Santa authority. This so upset me that I asked my mom to confirm Santa's authenticity. Her response was a simple: "Son, as long as you believe in Santa, there will be a Santa." Based on my insatiable need for toys, I decided it best to side with mom.

Got me to thinking ..... there is no way that fat dude could slide down our chimney. Something didn't fit. The story was contradictory at best. The deal was if you were a good boy Santa would bring toys. Fact is I was not a good boy. Heck, I chewed gum during class, aggravated all the neighborhood girls and often shot the wrong things with my BB rifle. Even with all this delinquency, I still got toys.

How could such an undeserving, mischievous kid like me get all the great toys, fruit and candy year after year. Furthermore, I knew of not a single kid who ever got coal or sticks - and believe me I knew some naughty kids. The whole Santa tale just seemed confusing, fictional and irrational at best.

As I have gotten older, and yes wiser, I have come to believe in Santa Claus. It has become easier to believe in the possibility of the grace and forgiveness offered by this Santa fellow once you meet Jesus.

As a Christian, I exalt Jesus Christ as my Lord and savior. I believe He loves and blesses me even though I fall short of His expectations. He gives me hope of life eternal although I disappoint Him frequently. I hope Santa is good to each of you this Christmas. I'm just thankful that Jesus comes more than once a year.

Big Men On Campus

All the ridiculous homage paid to professional athletes these days reminds me of three high schools friends. They were James, Harold and Kenneth Graham, three brothers from a poor black family. They were quiet, polite and never involved in any extra-curricular activities. They had to work in the afternoons to help their parents make ends meet plus they had no after school transportation.

In today's world, they would have no reason to be humble - they were incredibly athletic. All three had bodies that were chiseled and strong as oxen. They never worked out or lifted weights, it was all natural.

James walked in the weight room one day at lunch and bench pressed 50 lbs more than the toughest stud on the football team. Kenneth ran the 100 yard dash under the school record time in PE one day in street shoes and 30 degree weather. I can remember the side seams unraveling on James' pants because his thighs were so enormous. They had the talent and ability to be "big men on campus" under today's standards.

Got me to thinking ….. the biggest, best and most capable are not always on center stage. Our world is overly consumed in celebrity, glamour and spotlight. The pathway to the top is much more dependent on promotion than ability. I sometimes wonder how the Graham brothers must have felt. If they were jealous, envious or sought attention, they never showed it.

Humility is not an option for us as Christians. It is an essential. Jesus praised the humble, the poor in spirit, the destitute. Scripture insists that we either walk humbly with Him, or not at all. Humility comes from seeing yourself in relation to God.

My biblical hero John the Baptist says it best, "He must increase, but I must decrease." I often think about the Graham boys. I wonder where they are and what they are doing. My regret is that I did not fully appreciate their humility back in those days. In hindsight they were "big men on campus."

One For The Birds

Biggie and I spent most of Saturday afternoon watching the bluebirds from the porch of the man cave. One thing we look forward to each spring around my house is watching the nesting activity of the bluebirds that populate our backyard. Biggie and I build their houses as well as provide food and water for the blue birds along with many other species of birds that make our Saturday afternoons enjoyable.

Being a blue bird landlord is a hobby enjoyed by many. Books have been written about these creatures and bluebird clubs are scattered across the country. Construction details for the blue houses are specific.

One detail is the size of the entry hole. It is to be 1 1/2 inches in diameter .... no smaller, no larger. The reason for the 1 1/2 entry hole is to prevent other birds from entering. Other birds such as starling, wrens or sparrows may enter the houses and nest themselves or destroy the nest already built by the bluebird.

Got me to thinking ..... do we build specific size holes of entry in our lives? Are we intentional about who and who we don't allow in our box? Surely we don't want the poor, hungry and naked entering into our space. Are we too concerned with who we are and what we look like that we have no tolerance for others among us?

Evaluate your guest list. Take a peek at your social calendar. Who do you allow in your life? Who is in your social circle? According to Isaiah, God will someday bring together people from every nation to live together under His lordship.

Wouldn't it be nice to be ahead of that curve and experience a taste of heaven here on earth? Wouldn't it be a good thing to communicate with, understand, and trust others who differ from us in culture and tradition .... ways that often divide? Biggie and I have decided the next box we build ...... we are building it with a bigger hole.

A Friend Says "Goodbye"

I have done it again. You would think I have learned by now. I have given my heart totally to a pet. He is an English bulldog named Preacher. I've had many pets over the years that provided me with trusted companionship and were special buddies for me beyond what any human could offer. The price paid is unbearable pain when faced with the loss of a special canine friend.

I lost my friend Biggie last year. He too was an English bulldog. I accepted his suffering until his quest for life was no match for his illness. When the final day came, I had to ask my wife to be with him in his final moment. I simply could not bear to be there.

I was with my Hannah, a beautiful boxer, in 2001 when death became a kinder option than the life she was living. I remember riding down the road and seeing a sign nailed to a tree that read "Boxer puppies $50.00" ..... I held her as she breathed her last breath. It was a moment that drained every emotion from my being. A portrait of Hannah hangs in our home. She will always be with us right there with Biggie. I was never much good at "good bye."

Got me to thinking ….. about Jon Tumilson. Jon was one of 30 Navy SEALs recently killed when a rocket-propelled grenade took out their Chinook helicopter. Tumlinson had given his heart to a Labrador retriever named Hawkeye. Hawkeye was such an important part of Tumlison's life that he called him "son." Hawkeye buried his friend last week. At the service attended by 1,500 family and friends, Hawkeye was there paying his last respects.

When a friend of Tumlinson walked to the front during the service to speak, Hawkeye followed. He approached the casket, dropped down with a heaving sigh and refused to leave the side of his fallen friend. Love as pure and uncompromising can only come from Jesus. When God commands that we love each other, He has an agenda.

Love softens hard people. Love makes impatient people wait. Love brings us into relationships that allow us to see the face of God. So true are the words of John 15:13: "Greater love has no man than to lay down his life for a friend." It is a special blessing when we are able to love such to realize that truth …… pets included.

You Are Wanted At Checkout One

There is a dangerous and deadly influenza spreading across the landscape of retail America. It threatens to close the doors of every Wal-Mart and Harris Teeter across our country.

The overall impact poses a significant threat of lost jobs, vacant buildings and scarcity of goods and products necessary for daily existence. The threat is being referred to as "closed checkout line itis." To look this beast in the eyes, simply visit a Wal-Mart or Harris Teeter for direct exposure.

As a business owner for over 25 years, I simply do not understand how merchants allow this to happen. To be successful, businesses must spend lots of money to get the customer in the door. They invest massive amounts of capital to build the building and stock the shelves. They build an employee base with commitments of payroll and benefit packages. Then at the finish line (check out line) they drop the ball.

Got me to thinking .... is this how we run our churches? Do we stock our shelves with worship services, small groups, mission opportunities and then drop the ball avoiding up close and personal follow up with the ones who choose to shop at our store. The church has long been marketed as a safe haven. Advertised as the place to come when you need help. The people's choice where the folks are nice and willing to sit with those who may be, or at least feel, undesirable. Are we so consumed with our projection screen, webinar and simulcast that we have no time to shake one another's hand?

Why is the church dying? We are doing a super job with promotion. You need someone to "cast a vision" just call on any church leader. The question is - are we following through with our enthusiasm until we make real and actual contact? Are we putting our hands and feet with the sermons and rhetoric?

God has already done all he needs to do for each of us to live free and victorious lives in Christ. What we sometimes overlook is our role and commitment to leave no one waiting in the checkout line.

Rather Have A Daughter

First let me say I do not have a daughter. I would not have been able to handle it especially if she looked like her mother. With that being said, let's say you have a daughter. She has just announced her plans to marry. You are sitting around chatting with your friends and you share the news. I guarantee you the first question they will ask is: "what does the young man do for a living?" What we do - our occupations - define us in the world.

We expect our doctor to have all the medical answers. We never hesitate in asking our mechanic to listen to the rattle in our engine and immediately offer a diagnosis. Surely our personal trainer has a quick and easy shortcut for us to lose weight and keep in shape. Our culture places significant demands on folks in regard to the shingle they hang outside their door.

One profession hit hard by our demands is the pastors in our churches. As our spiritual leaders, they are expected to hold the miracle working powers of Jesus himself. They constantly deal with pain, brokenness and despair. There are more funerals in the life of a preacher than weddings.

Got me to thinking ….. pastors are normal human beings. They need real, normal friends. They need confidants, and relationships built on things other than church. When is the last time you invited your pastor over for dinner or to a movie? They enjoy the same things you and I enjoy.

When is the last time you told them you appreciated them rather than complaining about the content of their sermon? Paul tells us in Thessalonians 5:12-13 to know and esteem our pastors.

From the time I attended church as a child til I stand before you today, I give thanks for the pastors that have guided and comforted me. Thanks be to God that He provides us with such people of courage. As for me? I couldn't handle the pressure, rather have a daughter.

Money Can Buy You Love

We have heard it all our lives ... "Money won't make you happy." The Beatles had a hit titled money "Can't Buy Me Love." With all due respect to the Liverpool lads, I beg to differ. Take Tina for example. She was my waitress at The Waffle House one morning last week in D'Iberville, Mississippi.

Tina's happiness was evidenced by a beautiful smile when she spoke about the money in relief donations that flowed into the Gulf Coast after Hurricane Katrina. That money, Tina referred to, represented survival, it represented hope, it brought relief.

You must first understand that Tina used to work in a doctor's office, a good paying job for those parts. Now she waits tables at The Waffle House. The doctor she worked for packed up and left the area after Katrina - his practice dried up. Money for Tina is a precious commodity considering her pre-Katrina apartment rent was $400 ..... now it's $850.

Got me to thinking ..... about the other side of life in storm torn Mississippi that we never see in the news headlines. Tina told the story of a brother who killed his sister over a bag of ice. $2.00 could have saved her life. She mentioned friends that have not been found and the realization that they are not coming back. She talked about how her elderly father was struggling to make ends meet fishing the waters of the Gulf Coast. She was appreciative of the aid that flowed after the storm but confirmed that the stream of money and volunteers had slowed to a trickle.

My friend Jon and I made a promise to Tina. We made a commitment to return and to bring money. That money will buy building materials - that money will pay apartment rent - that money will repair lives.

Contrary to the lyrics of the Fab Four .... in time and places of brokenness, money and the service in which it is offered can buy you love. My friends did in fact return. ...... they brought money. Just ask Tina. You can find her at The Waffle House with a smile.

Home

My wife and son were away last week visiting friends in Boston. I had the entire house to myself. The absence of others provided unfamiliar quiet time and relaxation. It's kinda odd how your home takes on a different personality when you are there alone. There's an added appreciation for the space. It seems bigger. You notice things you missed before.

Home is a big deal. You know ...... "there is no place like home" .... "home is where the heart is." Being "homeward bound" is always a good thing. For some, home may be a cardboard box, backseat of a car or an office. For others it is a prison, elderly care facility or a rehab center.

I think about people who move frequently like missionaries, military people or those in transient type careers. They have many homes over their lifetime. The rich and famous have multiple homes ... on the coast, in the mountains and abroad.

I believe that God has chosen a magnificent home for His people. In this place, we will see the heart of our Father and witness the completed redemption of His people. In this home, we will be reunited with loved ones. There will be no pain and suffering.

Got me to thinking .... to be home is what we all long for, and that is what all who know Jesus Christ as Lord and Savior will have .... an eternal place to dwell. I heard a loud voice shout from the throne saying, "Look, God's home is now among His people. He will live with them and they will be His people" (Revelation 21:3).

Well, they are home now. The noise is back ..... the reflective state of solitude is gone .... the quiet refuge is just a memory. Phones are ringing, doors are slamming, dogs are barking .... life as I know and love has returned. The travelers missed home and home missed the travelers.

Paradise

Sometimes a song gets stuck in my heart. The lyrics become something for me possibly contrary to the intentions of the artist. I write my own song with the lyrics. The lyrics of the early tunes by James Taylor were written while "Sweet Baby James" was committed to a mental institution addicted to heroin. Consider the conditions under which the beautiful lyrics of "Carolina On My Mind" were penned. Even though the words of "Imagine" were a product of John Lennon who announced his popularity exceeded that of Christ, they strike a deeply spiritual place in my heart.

My point is ..... regardless of the intentions of the writer, song lyrics can speak to us in ways we choose. Such a song for me is the tune by Coldplay titled "Paradise." In the song a girl "expects the world" but it "flew away from her reach." Her "tears become a waterfall" as she "flew away in the stormy night."

Got me to thinking ..... these lyrics could be overlaid upon many circumstances folks face in today's world of challenge, pain and loss. My easy grooved enjoyment of the song is derailed by being reminded of all the world's suffering. Like the girl in the song, I too "close my eyes at night and dream of paradise." I call it prayer.

The melodies, rhythm and music of this tune are relaxing and smoothly flowing but the lyrics are raw and desolate. I am constantly reminded that we all carry a burden. Everyone, regardless of their outward appearance, is struggling inside with either self induced or connected pain.

In the song, the girl "knows the sun must set to rise." These lyrics speak of hope. "Life goes on" wails Coldplay front man, Chris Martin. As Christians, the struggles we face are manageable because of our faith.

Our future is founded on the rock we know as Jesus. Life moves with the assurance that He who created us has "prepared a place for us." For now we'll call it "Paradise."

Keep Your Eye On The Road

I live in a neighborhood where the roads are winding and the terrain is rolling and hilly. There are locations where only a few feet separate the road's edge from a fifty feet drop in elevation. Just imagine a roller coaster with a steering wheel. With all this being said, my son received his driver's license last week, so keep our family and neighbors in your prayers.

There is another challenge associated with our roads. To heighten the danger of the shifting terrain and blind curves, there are no lines on the roadway. No center lane divider line or shoulder marker lines.

The risk associated with the absence of the lines is played out on a daily basis with multiple near misses from cars rounding curves only to find an approaching vehicle encroaching on its space. It is obvious that many drivers, at least drivers that frequent or visit our neighborhood, need some visible parameters.

Got me to thinking ..... where would I be headed without the marker lines represented by Jesus in my life. The short answer is "in the ditch." The demons in today's world are well hidden. Pride, envy, jealousy and lust are just a few of the serpents hidden under the rocks of life ready to strike. The battle between good and evil within every Christian is real. Check out Romans 7:14-25 for Paul's take on that. Conflict between our sinful nature and what Jesus wants us to be is played out constantly in our relationships at home, work and yes ...... among fellow believers.

What a blessing when Jesus becomes the marker lines in our life. His spirit reminds us, encourages us, loves and forgives us as we navigate the winding, rolling and twisting highways of life. Good defense strategy when brokenness, loss and defeat blur our vision and tempt to derail our travel.

God is our road marker. He is our beacon, our GPS. He is our rest stop. It is in Him that we find our destination. It is within His lines of holiness that we navigate through and around the reality of our own ungodliness. Safe travels to all.

Words

I was with a young couple last week. They were overflowing with joy. Their child had just spoken his first word. His first word was "ball." His dad is convinced that junior is destined to be a professional baseball player. I assured the parents the novelty of his chatter would rapidly disappear.

God spoke the first words. Those words set creation in motion. Words belong to the Lord. In today's culture, words are mundane. We simply think of words as tools to make our lives easier and more efficient.

The book of Proverbs suggests that words either give life; or bring death - we choose when we speak. You have never spoken a neutral word in your life. All words have an agenda. Words of encouragement, love, peace, unity and hope are words of life. Words of slander gossip, judgment, anger and contempt are words of death.

Got me to thinking ….. our ability to speak is something most of us take for granted. Sitting with my dad after he was afflicted with Alzheimer's gave me a different take on speech. I now reflect and cherish the memories of our past conversations.

His voice was like no other to me. Kinda like the sheep and shepherd relationship we read about in the book of John. I did not hear him speak a single word the last year of his life. How I missed that dimension of our relationship.

There are over one million words in the English language. On average, folks know an estimated 20,000 and use 2,000 a week. Remember, the words you speak go off into eternity. With so much at stake may your words be seasoned with kindness and grace.

A Temple Is Built In Africa

Second Chronicles Chapters 3-4 describes the temple built during King Solomon's reign. The materials used were the finest available and the craftsmanship and skill of the workers was second to none. There were jewel studded walls, doors overlaid with gold and an altar made of bronze.

Scripture tells us when the temple was dedicated; God's presence was so thick among the people that "the priests could not perform their service for the glory of the Lord filled the temple of God." My son and I were part of a team that recently built a home. The lumber was rough cut and warped. The roof was sheet tin and the floor was hand mixed concrete. The labor force was unskilled.

The home was being built for Hemme, a teenage girl orphaned by the AIDS epidemic in Africa. The two room 15X 24 dwelling would provide a home for Hemme and her 15 year old brother. Like the temple, once completed, the home was dedicated. There were people from the local church and neighborhood in attendance to join in the celebration of this wonderful blessing.

We all laid hands on the dwelling as prayers were offered up and songs were sung. Just as with the temple dedication, the spirit of our Lord was thick among the people present.

Got me to thinking ….. Jesus teaches that poverty, hunger, homelessness and medical epidemics should be concerns of the redeemed. Social and cross cultural investment ought to be important to every follower of Christ. The love shown to our brothers and sisters in need emulates God's love and is eternally transforming.

Service to God involves doing the best you can with the materials and skill sets you have. Jesus reminds us that whatever we do, we must work at it with all our hearts, as working for the Lord, not for men. Whether it's a magnificent temple or a humble homestead, it all matters to God.

Rebel With A Cause

Many of the images coming across the nightly news recently have been alarming. We have seen deadly force being used against the people of Libya as they gather in protest against their ruthless leader Muammar al-Gaddafi. Gaddafi was categorized in a newspaper article as wily, eccentric and shrewd. Let's just say the editor was kind.

Inspiration for the Libyan uprising is attributed to the recent unrest in Egypt. Overall what we see occurring in the Middle East and North Africa is no longer a protest movement, it's a war. It's open revolt.

It's a shame to see innocent folks slaughtered in the streets by the institutions and agencies that should be protecting them. While we are many times frustrated with our government and the leaders that make daily decisions that affect our lives, just a viewing of the nightly news should make us thankful that things are more in control in our neighborhood. Aside from the politics, I can't help thinking about Jesus while digesting these images.

Got me to thinking ….. Jesus was an unintentional political rebel. His mission of proclaiming the reign of God had profound political implications. Our Lord was not crucified for teaching love and forgiveness or debating legal points with the scribes of the day. Jesus was crucified because he was seen as a threat to the powers in charge. His brand of nonviolent resistance, his manner of stirring the people and empowering the poor, challenged the Gaddafi's and Mubarak's of the day.

The crucifixion of Jesus should always be seen in the context of how he lived his life. Jesus had no political aspirations. He lived a risky life, took a dangerous path, attacked power and wealth. He overturned social attitudes, talked about prayer, service and love for your neighbor. He called people to freedom and empowerment in the face of injustice. He called the religious elite "vipers" for sponging off the poor.

Jesus laid it all on the line. He knew the risk. Seeking no political gain or fortune, He traveled a path that lead Him to death on a cross. Our indebtedness for sin was paid on that day …. all politics aside.

Just Say It ... I Love You

Folks speak all the time about reading the book - you know - the Bible. They boast "I've read it cover to cover" .... Genesis to Revelation. Many commit to the "cover to cover" journey each year. As Christians, we know that reading and studying God's word is the most necessary foundational component in our spiritual formation. I can personally testify that my participation in Disciple Bible Study over the years has been the basis for my true appreciation and understanding of God's word. It is the centerpiece of our faith journey.

With that being said, what I have gathered the book is telling me from "cover to cover" is to LOVE. Love one another. Love our enemies. Love the poor. Love the needy. And love God like no other. Got me to thinking .... I just sent an e-mail to a MAN and finished with "I love you." WOW - that is a stretch for a full blooded, conservative, southern boy to say to another man.

"I love you" is a difficult, "lump in the throat", kinda thing for some folks to say to anyone. Wouldn't it be a better world somehow if we all had the courage to speak love to those in our lives? When my parents passed there were no regrets. I NEVER left them without saying "I love you." I would be in agony today if I had been too shy to express my love for them. Yes - they knew it but it must have been "heaven" for them to hear those words from their son.

Got me to thinking ….. life is just too short for us to leave anything hanging. Just say it "I Love You." Remember that "cover to cover" stuff. It's all about love. When we invite God into our heart, we are inviting His love to assume absolute priority. What good is that love if we choose not to express it.

I was with my oldest son recently on a church work project. When the work was completed and the day was spent, we headed in separate directions. Before our departure he said: "Dad, see you later - I love you." I hope and trust he meant it but it sure felt like "heaven" to hear him say it.

Survivor

Our family has been searching for an English bulldog puppy since the beginning of December. I was hoping to have one sitting in my lap on Christmas morning but it was not to be. We have talked to breeders from Raleigh to California. This breed is scarce compared to some other breeds and somewhat hard to find.

I have learned a great deal about dogs and breeders through this process ..... some things good - some things not so good. One breeder told the story of a recent litter being killed by their mother. I don't understand this phenomenon nor do I care to. Regardless of any physiological explanation, it's just not right - it's not natural. Mothers are supposed to love their children and it is an unbearable state of affairs when things go this wrong. A puppy should feel secure cuddled close to its mother and certainly not fear for its life.

Got me to thinking ..... about the gospel of Mark, 6th chapter. Here we see Jesus being devoured by his own people. Even though Jesus grew up in Nazareth in a well respected family, he found himself among detractors. His own community was amazed that this man who grew up as a carpenter was performing miracles among the people. Heck, he had never attended a rabbinical school ...... he needed to stick to making tables, chairs and repairing farming tools.

Our lives in this world are tightly wrapped in blankets of irony. A world where Christians argue, disagree, accuse and compete with one another, and mama dogs kill their young. If others choose not to respect your Christian work, don't let their rejection keep you from serving God.

Just before sending this message my wife and I returned from Asheville. We traveled to meet a breeder midway from western Tennessee. Nothing like sharing the backseat with a new friend, two survivors beginning a journey together.

Costly Forgiveness

Need a sermon on forgiveness? If so, I highly recommend the story of Rachelle Friedman. Just days before Rachelle was scheduled to be married, she was paralyzed in poolside horseplay at her bachelorette party. The accident was a result of a bridesmaid friend pushing Rachelle into the pool and her landing awkwardly on the shallow cement bottom.

I can only imagine how I would have reacted. Wedding cancelled, future uncertain, the reality of living life confined to a wheelchair and especially the hatred for the one who was to blame. But not Rachelle.

She has stood by her friend as newspapers, television and Internet sites have carried the story around the world. Rachelle admits that it could just have easily been her who pushed her friend in the pool. She associates the incident as something that happened to both the girls.

Got me to thinking ….. forgiveness is not an easy thing. Our natural instinct is to recoil in self protection when we have been injured. It is not natural to overflow with mercy, grace and forgiveness when bad things happen to you at the hands of others. Forgiveness is a choice we make through a decision of our will. As Christians, this choice is motivated by obedience to God and his command to forgive others as we seek forgiveness.

Rachelle has since married. Things were a little different than first planned. Instead of walking her down the aisle, her father piloted her wheelchair. What did not change was that her friend was there with her as a bridesmaid.

I do not know Rachelle or anything about her faith. What I do know is she has lived Colossians 3:13 in testimony to the world that we can forgive even when the cost is high. I have a very special person in my life that is wheelchair bound and is at peace with his life. I could not help but think of him when I read of Rachelle. It sounds like she must be special like him. Because of him I can relate and celebrate her story. May God bless them both.

The Wicked Witch Is Dead

Those of my generation surely remember the Wizard of OZ. While created in 1939, it was not until 1956 that the film was broadcast to the public. The film became an annual tradition winning two Academy Awards and a nomination for Best Picture of the Year. For us pre-video, pre-DVD, pre-Bluetooth crowd, it was a horror flick, action adventure and Broadway musical all wrapped into one.

One of my favorite scenes was when Dorothy's house, lifted by a tornado, landed atop the Wicked Witch of the East. There was something extra victorious about extreme evil meeting its match. While she was frightened and relieved, Kansas farm girl Dorothy was almost saddened. She even commented to the Wicked Witch of the West that she had nothing to do with the tragedy. Got to say I kinda had a Dorothy moment upon learning of the death of Muammar Gaddafi.

It was akin to the conflicting sensation of celebration and concern I felt when Saddam Hussein and Osama Bin Laden bit the dust. As news of Gaddafi's death spread, people poured into the streets. His 42 year reign of terror was over. Drug from a sewer pipe and shot in the head with his own pistol made of gold, weaves a webbed eulogy of sarcasm and irony.

Got me to thinking ….. about Proverbs 28:15 "Like a roaring lion or a charging bear is a wicked ruler over a poor people." Jesus further instructs in Matthew 26:52 to put away the sword saying "Those who use the sword will die by the sword."

Bin Laden, Hussein and Gaddafi all wielded their sword against the poor and will have to answer for their actions and face whatever judgment God has for them.

I hope, as I find myself humming "Ding Dong the Witch is Dead," that God will help me reconcile in my heart the love and forgiveness that He expects of me for these deceased evil ones.

Holier Than Thou

I was behind a garbage truck one morning last week. The truck was stopping along the street emptying the cans that had been rolled to the curb. The frequent stops by the truck had created a small traffic backup.

The traffic jam was normal considering the nature of the job. What I didn't expect was the behavior of some of the folks in the traffic jam. They were blowing their horns, making various hand gestures and attempting to dangerously pass the stopped garbage truck. Man !!!!! - I thought I was in New Jersey for goodness sakes.

Chances are the folks that were raising such a fit had recently had their can emptied and through that process some other persons might have been slowed or stopped in traffic. But that does not matter. It is all about US. It is all about OUR time. So what if someone had to wait for my trash to be collected. I do not have time to wait for theirs.

Sometimes this is how Christians can be - heck we are only human. I think there is especially a tendency to be impatient with non-believers.

All of a sudden we are Holy and don't have time for those unchurched "heathens". Research shows that many non believers reject Jesus because they feel rejected by Christians. This is so unfortunate. One nonbeliever was quoted as saying "Christianity has become so bloated with blind followers who would rather repeat slogans and quote scripture than extend true compassion and love."

Got me to thinking ..... about the story of a church that limited the printing of announcements in the church bulletin to only subjects that affected the "majority" of the congregation. What about the "minority." We all were there once.

As transformed people, God has picked up our trash from the curb. We must always be sensitive to those whose garbage is still awaiting the truck. Let's not be hindered by being more focused on our holiness than the unholiness of others in our midst.

Friends

This facebook craze amazes me. I am not a regular but it's kinda neat to connect with friends that I might not be able to otherwise. Yes, I said friends. One interesting thing about facebook is the concept of friend. You are invited to be someone's friend. Currently I have 178 - no wait a minute - 179 friends on facebook. I just had another request. Some of these facebook friends I don't know very well but how can I deny their request to be my friend?

Friendship to me is a serious thing. I expect alot from a friend and in return I try to give alot to my friends. There is however a reality to friendships. All the time, precious time, we spend with friends ought to be something that lasts. Well - it doesn't. Friends die, friends change, friends move away.

Found out last week that I am losing one of my dearest friends. He is moving away to greener pastures. I am both happy for and very proud of him. We have talked and agreed to stay connected but the reality is that things will not be the same. He gave me an old worn out golf cap he wears. I will hang the cap in my man cave. We've spent alot of time in that place and the hat will be a great reminder of the good ole days.

Got me to thinking ..... accumulate all the friends you can on facebook, that's a good thing. But also invest the time, patience and understanding that is required to cultivate some deep and wide relationships.

Give of yourself and sacrifice your secrets to those willing to share the like with you. Don't keep count because true friendship is precious and the number of true friends you have may be only single digit.

**Greater love hath no man than this,
that a man lay down his life for his friends**

John 15: 13

Burnout

I recently attended a men's rally where the keynote speaker shared his personal testimony. He alluded to his experience in the church as a child. He and his brothers were just youngsters, when their family left the organized church because their dad was completely burned out. His dad was active and involved in every aspect of service within their church to the point of neglecting his own life in Christ as well as his family.

His dad's decision to leave the church lead to circumstances that later prompted his dropping out of school and both his brothers becoming drug addicts. It's easy to have our energies revolve around activities for Christ instead of around Christ himself.

The particulars of this story that happened some thirty years ago still continue in our churches today. This ongoing cycle of burnout does achieve measurable and tangible stuff like congregational growth, big numbers for small group meetings and Bible studies as well as zombie disciples.

Got me to thinking …. about Exodus 18:18 where Moses was warned that his failure to delegate authority would wear himself and his people out. The story told by the speaker was unfortunate. The wounding of his dad had repercussions that were passed on to future generations.

The good news is that our speaker was committed to breaking the cycle. Burnout is a product of the dark side we face as Christians in our attempt to serve Jesus. It is important to be aware of this trap and strive to achieve balance in our lives.

The key to achieving and maintaining balance in our lives is trusting God. It is important to always remember that our life is a gift from God and what we do with our lives is our gift back to Him. Passing on responsibilities and delegating to others can be a gift in itself.

It's not wise to burn our candles at both ends. Sometimes we have to say no in order to say yes.

The Preacher

It's gonna be a long spring and summer. Our family, we are outdoor folks. On any given weekend my son is hitting golf balls, mom is planting flowers and I am riding some form of machinery over the five acres where we live. It's our release. It has been my practice to have a companion in my endeavors .... more specifically an English bulldog.

I lost a great yard mate, "Biggie" last year. He knew the drill. After a couple of laps around the yard he settled down in the shade and napped the day away. I miss that fellow. We recently brought a new one into our family ... his name is "Preacher."

Preacher and I had our first work day on Saturday. If I may repeat myself, it's gonna be a long spring and summer. Preacher was everywhere ..... chasing the tractor, running away with yard tools and licking me in the face as I stood on my head spreading pine straw. When the time came to clean the koy fish ponds .... you guessed it .... he took a swim.

Got me to thinking ..... about an elderly friend of mine who recently offered some words of wisdom:

"Do it now while you can." What he was saying was don't wait. "There will come a time when your current abilities will leave you and will not return." That was a truth with somewhat haunting reality.

As I expressed my frustrations throughout the day on Saturday, my wife reminded me that the day will come when this bundle of energy we call Preacher will be old and slow. She suggested I enjoy and celebrate his energy while he had it. There needs to be a sense of urgency in our lives as we serve our Lord. When Jesus said "come and follow me" ...... well last time I checked, "follow" is a verb.

Remember ... when your life flashes before your eyes make sure you've got plenty to watch. It's gonna be a long spring and summer ..... can't wait !!!!!

Back Porch Demons

Growing up we had a screened porch on the side entrance of our home. We lived on a farm so this area was filled with fresh vegetables just picked from the garden, muddy boots, buckets and the like. There was a shelf built around three walls about 18 inches from the ceiling.

Since the shelf was high, there were "dangerous things" kept there, things that a child had no business bothering. One such item was a can of RED DEVIL lye. Back in those days lye was somewhat of a household item around the farm and for those not familiar with the stuff ...... it ain't baking soda.

On the can was a large image of Lucifer himself. Quite a frightening image for a youngster. Whenever I would enter the porch at night, I would not look up at the shelf as I ran to the safety of the adjoining kitchen. On the rare occasions that I would look up at the can, it seemed as though the ole devil himself was staring me straight in the eyes.

Got me to thinking ….. I am no longer afraid of that can. Yes, I recognize the devil is a fallen but powerful spirit presenting himself in many forms.

Greed, envy, lust, love of money and ego are just a few of his disguises. He is smart. Just as soon as we take a stand for Jesus, he turns up the volume in his efforts to tempt and derail our faith journey.

While we need to be aware of this threat, Lucifer should not be our focus. We should always look to God instead. He will provide a protective hedge around us to empower our resistance. However, we can't underestimate this adversary. He is real, he is crafty, he is dangerous. More times than not, we will not recognize him.

Don't look for the guy on the lye can - he is far too smart for that. When he comes disguised as temptation, flee him and don't leave a forwarding address. He may win a few battles but Jesus assures us he will not win the war.

Tim Tebow

It has taken some time but I have finally come around to agree with all the NFL experts that claim Tim Tebow doesn't have the ingredients to be a star NFL quarterback. He doesn't have a reality show star girlfriend or has he yet to finance an illegal dog fighting ring. He's an oddball. Please understand, there are many fine young men at the quarterback position in the NFL but Tim Tebow sets a new standard.

There are many who take the responsibility as role models seriously and set the bar high regarding moral character and behavior becoming a gentleman. But to me, none like this young man who spends his off season in the mission fields.

After becoming the starting quarterback, Tebow lead the Denver Broncos to their first playoff berth since 2005. Even with this record he has taken criticism regarding his play and apparent "obsession with Jesus." Even professing believers are critical of his trademark praise to God after big plays and at game's end. It has been suggested that he "back off the Jesus talk." Tebow has stood firm in his faith.

Got me to thinking ….. Jesus himself was met with a challenging community. His ministry was seemingly unappreciated. He was mimicked and mocked. With that being said, Hebrews 4:2 teaches that "our faith does us no good unless we share it with others." Further in Matthew 5:15 we are cautioned not to light a lamp and put it under a bowl. Instead we are to put it on a stand so it gives light to everyone in the house.

We could only hope that all our young people, especially those of celebrity, could possess the courage of Tim Tebow. He did not ask for all this hype or to stand in the national spotlight. He has not sold out to all the worldly temptations that fall at his feet on a daily basis. He, like all of us, has been called to be an ambassador for Christ.

Jesus called out: "come follow me and I will show you how to fish for people." I saw a quote the other day that says it best: "Our faith when unshared is like a glove without a hand .... lifeless."

Thank you Tim Tebow for putting your hand in the glove of your faith for all to see regardless of what the world thinks. I am confident I speak for Christians around the world when I say: "we got your back" !!!!

When Our Young Pass

I left for work earlier than usual one day last week. Traffic was a little different, specifically there were school buses. First I squirmed and became agitated at the frequent stops and slow movement of traffic. After a few minutes of elevated blood pressure I began to watch the children waiting beside the road to catch their ride to school.

It was cold and they were bundled up and covered beyond recognition. They were wrapped in hoodies, ski jackets and gloves as foggy clouds swirled from their mouths with each breath. All of a sudden I had plenty of time.

As a buddy of mine used to say, "our children carry our hearts." There is no greater gift from God than our children. We see ourselves in their faces, attitudes and actions. We love them unconditionally and spend abundant time in prayer asking God to watch over them. We make sacrifices for them. We prioritize our lives for them.

Our children provide us as parents the awesome opportunity of adorning our parents as grandparents.

Two families I know have lost children recently. This is truly a time of challenge. When a child passes, we lose our rational, reasonable, sensible faith in the way life is supposed to work. It always catches us off guard. When a child is lost we suddenly have no plans. Our dreams are shattered. Lost is our understanding of life's rhythm and purpose. Our children are supposed to bury us.

Got me to thinking .... how Jesus wept as they placed Lazarus in the tomb. He wept and allowed himself to be caught up in the intense emotion of the moment while at the same time knowing He would raise him from the dead. The assurance of resurrection is what we embrace as Christians during such tragic times. These children are now in a place apart from all the pain and challenge this world provides.

Nothing prepares us for the death of a child. God handles all those details. Left for those behind is a faith based promise of a soon to be grand reunion.

Character Reference

Recently I've been asked by several people to act as a character reference for them. A couple of the requests were for jobs, one was for a security clearance and another was part of an application process for entry into Asbury Seminary. WOW !!!!!! this is big stuff.

My first response was how touching it was for someone to think that another they needed to impress would value my opinion (hope that came out right). Once I got through the first few seconds of pride, I entered into a deeper appreciation of friends that would bestow upon me such an honor.

Got me to thinking ….. a person would call you into this role only if they were confident that you knew the "good" things they had to offer and you were willing to share that with others. They are hedging, betting and hoping that they have so impressed you with their "goodness" that you would be willing to celebrate that with others. Wonder if Jesus would use me as a reference?

Many people in today's culture have grown cynical about religion. Our country is at war, our economy is in the tank, gangs are taking over our schools. There has never been a greater need in this world for Christ. We all have been called upon by Jesus as references.

Are you willing and prepared to act as a reference for Christ? Can you testify to His message and values? I am not referring to the transactions we engage in on Sunday within the walls of our church. I'm talking about a public proclamation.

There is absolutely no question whether you are on the reference list - be unconditionally assured that you are. Step up and help out a brother from Nazareth. Eternal lives are at stake. One belongs to you.

Glass Houses

Tony Campolo is a favorite author of mine. I have heard him speak and read all of his books. One of my favorite Tony stories is when he was speaking to a group of pastors shortly after the Jim Bakker controversy. As he was introducing Campolo, the master of ceremonies said: "We must distance ourselves from the likes of Jim Bakker. Men like this have disgraced the church, and we must make it clear to our people that we are not like that."

Campolo was infuriated with the comments and began his talk with these words: "The difference between Jim Bakker and the rest of us is that they haven't found out about the rest of us yet. This is no time to distance ourselves from Bakker, but to acknowledge that what was in him is in all of us. Each of us has a dark side and if the truth were known, each of us would have to run away and hide."

Got me to thinking ….. what Jesus has done in my life does not make me a better person than you, but it does make me a better person than I was. In Galatians we find a reminder that when anyone is overtaken with fault, we must focus on restoration. We must look in the mirror knowing that somewhere down the line each of us will need restoring.

The line that separates good from evil does not separate one group of people from another. It runs right down the middle of each of us. There is certainly enough evil in the best of us and enough good in the worst of us not to look down on others. Be reminded that Christians sometimes spend too much energy telling folks what they are doing wrong instead of celebrating what they are doing right. Extending a hand is always better than pointing a finger.

Live creatively, friends. If someone falls into sin, forgivingly restore him, saving your critical comments for yourself. You might be needing forgiveness before the day's out. Stoop down and reach out to those who are oppressed. Share their burdens, and so complete Christ's law. If you think you are too good for that, you are badly deceived.
(Galatians 6:1-3)

The Needy Among Us

I was in the middle of a couple of situations last week. I find myself in situations all the time. Sometimes I learn from these situations and come out the other side enlightened. Sometimes confirmation of what we suspect is found within situations. I suggest such a confirmation is the face of the needy in today's world has changed. The economic environment that has caged many of us the past several years has produced an unfamiliar profile.

While what we consider the typical face of need, the homeless, unemployed etc still exists, there is a new category of folks who have fallen victim to foreclosure, bankruptcy and thus depression. These folks appear just fine on the outside but inside fight a battle and struggle with situations they are unprepared to handle. Not only must they face the banker, they also fall prey to the reality of their situation.

As they struggle with pride and embarrassment, they find themselves in a place they have never been before. They believed if they worked hard and lived right, things would be OK.

Our world has changed dramatically in the last 45 years. Our homes are bigger and our cars are more expensive. We have developed an insatiable appetite for high tech, high dollar stuff. While income for the average American has reached new heights, so has their comfort with debt. We now have an estimated 47.4 million poor in our country. That represents 15.8% of the population. The new poor are a well educated, hard working group that once experienced success but now stare hopeless failure in the face.

Got me to thinking ..... who are these people? Well - they are our neighbors, our friends and our family. They are sitting beside us in church. It is important that we expand our minds, and more importantly our hearts, to include these that find themselves in need.

Yea, we can say they have been reckless, greedy, unwise and irresponsible BUT does that make them less worthy of our hearts? As we enter into our true role of service to others, may we re-evaluate the face of the needy among us and act accordingly.

Flu Shot Ain't Enough

It's that time of year. My wife has begun to refine her strategy to persuade, trap and convince me to get a flu shot. It is estimated that 20% of Americans get the influenza vaccination each year. It has been a fundamental purpose of my better half to increase that percentage each year by one person ..... me. Our son, bless his heart, has no say. He is rushed down to our local CVS day one and stuck with the proverbial needle.

The wide spread use of the influenza vaccine dates back to research conducted in 1931 at Vanderbilt University. In the 1940's, the US military developed a vaccine based on this research that was widely used in World War II. The basic concept involves injecting inactivated flu virus (getting stuck with a needle) that will then stimulate the body to develop antibodies to fight off the illness when it strikes. That's as good of an explanation as you are gonna get from me. Cliff notes version ...... you get a little bit so you won't get a lot.

Got me to thinking ..... do we seek a vaccine - just a little dose of Jesus - with expectations it will cover all

He requires? Maybe if we go to church then we are covered. Get paid, pay our bills, indulge our needs and put what's left in the plate. We just as soon not give up things that may conflict with our worldly plans and desires.

Sounds a lot like the story of the man in Mark 10:21, wouldn't the vaccination of obeying the laws cover him from the sacrificial disease of selling it all and following Jesus completely? Vaccines are good things. They appear to be a great way to fight the flu but a lousy way to follow Jesus.

There is no shortcut to the suffering and sacrifice that is required of a disciple of Jesus Christ. There is no preventative measure for the ridicule and denial that comes with the territory. To live for Jesus requires the end of your life in the world. Open wide ...... take your medicine. An eternal cure will be your reward - no vaccine required.

Kay

Recently a friend of my wife passed on to her eternal home. Her name was Kay. My wife and Kay were childhood friends from grade school through college. They had a lot in common. Both were middle age with presumably their best years ahead, both were mothers to adolescence sons. My wife, when learning of Kay's death, wept uncontrollably. It's painful to watch those you love cry.

I did not know Kay well having met her only a couple of times. What I knew of her I gleaned from my wife. I did receive the blessing of exchanging an e-mail with her after she became ill. I know her faith was strong. She was a beautiful woman who took care of her husband and son as well as herself. She was a nonsmoker so it seemed senseless that lung cancer would take her from us.

I have struggled with her death. I watched my wife and her friends ride the roller coaster of emotion over the past year as they followed the surgeries and chemo treatments.

Got me to thinking …. this could have been my wife. I could be the widower. My son could be without a mother. How selfish of me. I have thought about Kay, her husband, Kevin and son, Andrew every day since Kay passed. My emotions have ranged from understanding to sorrow, from reflection to prayer, from questions to answers. I have thought about death, family, faith and salvation.

In worship this week we sang "How Great Thy Art." Hadn't sang that one in awhile. There it was in the second verse: **When God shall come with shouts of acclamation to take me home, what joy shall fill my heart. Then I shall bow in humble adoration and then proclaim my God how great thy art.**

At that very moment as I sang those words my struggle with Kay's untimely death was over. I was overcome with emotion. God had spoke to me through those lyrics. He told me that He had come for Kay. Being the almighty physician, the lady loved by many was now healed. No longer in pain, separated for eternity from suffering. The cancer did not win. Our God - how truly great thou art.

American Idol

Unless you've been living under a rock, you are familiar with the name, Scotty McCreery. Scotty is the teenager from Garner who won the American Idol contest. As a result of his "Idol" success, Scotty has become an overnight star with crowds of fans following him wherever he goes. Just this past weekend there was a parade and several special events in the Triangle area to celebrate the hometown celebrity.

While preparing for an upcoming speaking engagement at Garner Baptist church this week, I talked to folks at the church who know Scotty. It appears that Scotty was raised in a Christian home and has a strong foundation of faith under his feet. In every photo I've seen, a cross is clearly displayed around his neck. I am told that Scotty is quick to mention his faith and gives credit for his success to Jesus Christ.

Got me to thinking ..... while none of us may not be in contention for the title "American Idol", we have the same opportunity as Scotty to profess our faith.

Teachers have their students - Managers have their workers - Parents have their children. We all have people who look to us for guidance, for knowledge, for an example. God is not impressed with fame. He does however rejoice when we use our influence to promote His kingdom here on earth.

Whether we are Scotty McCreery or John Doe, we all have the opportunity and responsibility to tell all those around us about Jesus. We do that in our spoken words, the compassion we offer our neighbor and the decisions we make every day in our lives to honor God.

Join me in lifting up this young man in prayer that he may fully execute the plan that God has for his life. It appears at this point that plan just might be a big one.

Know Your Stuff

What a celebration that all the responsibilities of shopping for the holidays are behind me. I am not a shopper. My wife would disagree but the reality is that I do shop, but usually for myself I hit the mall with a well devised strategy intended to have me in and out fast with focused precision. I cringe thinking of sitting on a mall bench while sweet thang shops til she drops.

My personal shopping, as you might expect, is for "guy" kinda things. What do I know, or want to know, about perfume or jewelry? It is absolutely amazing at the number of folks working as salespeople who have no clue about the product they are peddling. More than once I heard excuses like "this is not my regular department" or "I am new here."

Got me to thinking ….. am I as prepared as I need to be when folks ask me about my faith? Am I equipped with all the right stuff to convince others that Jesus Christ has transformed my life? As Christians, we are commanded to share our faith with others. Our testimony and witness is the outward evidence of this spirit we claim Holy.

It is important to be prepared when someone asks "what is this Jesus thing all about?" Your response just may be the difference in encouraging a seeker to dig in their heels and learn more. When you believe in something, the evidence is apparent in your speech and your actions.

We don't have to stand on street corners and pass out pamphlets. Others should see Jesus in our love for others, our commitment to service as well as our divine elasticity when confronted with temptation and evil.

2 Corinthians 5:20 reminds us of the privilege of being an ambassador for God. Scripture says our role is as God was making his appeal through us. This is a huge responsibility that requires our very best preparation and effort. We should fulfill this obligation as if lives depended on it .... they do.

Sunday Visits

Many of my fondest childhood memories stem from the "visiting" my family did on Sunday afternoons. We would load up the Chevy Nova station wagon and off we would go to the home of friends and family. For me these trips usually involved climbing trees, raiding the watermelon patch or grape vineyard, shooting BB guns or riding the go-carts and motorcycles with my cousins.

What I cherish most as I grow older from those "visits" was the conversation. The grown-ups did most of the talking but the information gleaned from the discussions far exceeded anything learned in school. The fellowship was enhanced by the environment considering a majority of these discussions were held on the front porch in a swing or rocking chair. Have you ever rocked on a cat's tail - well - that's another story.

Today we have reason to think this basic and beautiful pleasure of conversation is being diminished. Jesus delved deeply into the pleasure of conversation. Truth is that many of His conversations were adversarial. His frequent opponents were the Pharisees, who were considered the best people of Jesus' time. He chose to make his moral arguments against the most moral of people. His criticism was often clever and biting. Jesus had the ability to say a lot in a few words.

Got me to thinking ….. about how conversation today, especially that of elected officials and self-appointed experts, seem to convey less substance while the number of words increase. There seems to be very few coming down from the sycamore tree and engaging in conversation that could lead them toward a new understanding of what they need to do with their life.

We live in a society that has grown very impersonal. Our kids are stowed away in upstairs play rooms being entertained by computer games or the internet. We don't talk - we don't visit. There is considerable value in sharing our presence with others that is being wastefully avoided. It's important that we visit others as well as open our own homes to our neighbors. Oh how I miss the Chevy Nova.

Cleo

I am a selfish person. Not proud of it - guess it's just part of my broken nature. I struggle with changing it every day. With God's help maybe one day I will be a better person in that regard.

It was a sad time in our house last week - we lost a family pet. She was a cat named Cleo. I am not a cat person but she was a good cat, as far as cats go. I admit I kinda shunned her and spent most of my pet time with our dogs.

She had a cancerous tumor and was very sick for several weeks. Only during this time did I come to appreciate her for the loyal companion she has been to our family. My wife rescued Cleo from a dumpster at Golden Corral sixteen years ago. She was an outdoor cat and earned her keep by relieving us of the occasional mouse or mole which she would proudly display at our back door.

She never sat perched on car hoods, sharpened her claws on the furniture or had a finicky nature like most cats. Shortly after Cleo came to live with our family, I purchased a chimenea for our patio. These are free standing ceramic fireplaces.

Before I had the opportunity to build my first fire, Cleo claimed it for her cat house. I always resented not being able, under orders from the wife, to use the chimenea in lieu of Cleo's choice of shelter. I always held that against her somehow (Cleo that is - not the wife.)

Got me to thinking ….. I am saddened by her passing. When the family hurts - I hurt regardless of the source of the pain. Sometimes we do not appreciate things until they are gone. One thing is for sure - there will never be a fire in the chimenea - it belongs to Cleo. Somehow I hope she understood my rude selfishness and long ago forgave me.

Death And Dying

I had my annual review with my cardiologist this week. This is an absolute event mandated by my wife, there is no discussion. She secretly checks my calendar, makes the appointment and informs me the night before so I can't wiggle out. Contrary to all evidence presented and with total disregard to rational reasoning, I think she loves me. The results of the visit were all good. She is happy and off my back for 364 days.

While I was on deck in a treatment room I could hear the doctor with another patient in the adjoining room. I could hear laughter which is a good sign. The news you get in these places is either good or not good. I could hear them talking but really wasn't paying attention until the end of the conversation. That's when I heard the doc say "I'll see you next year."

Got me to thinking ….. will the patient or doctor live to see another visit. A doctor friend of mine who makes his living putting people back together in the emergency room told me something interesting awhile back. His comment was "people do not believe they are going to die." He often sees repeat offenders who make return visits to his place all beaten and battered by careless and reckless lifestyles. Drunk drivers continue to crash their cars. Even after they are diagnosed with lung cancer, people continue to smoke. Victims of liver disease continue to do drugs.

Whether we are careless or submit to appropriate healthy behavior we are going to die. In Christ we find a strategy to face death head on. We turn from mourning death as the end to celebrating it as the beginning. With this being said, facing the fact of life's brevity may encourage each of us to do a better job in living the time God has allotted us.

We need to take care of our bodies in order to physically and mentally position ourselves to be the best we can be while here in this world. God expects that from each of us and it keeps our loved ones off our backs as well.

Are You A Fan

Been in a Christian bookstore lately? Most of the large chain stores have a great selection of books and "stuff." There is everything from a Jesus baseball cap to a Jesus food bowl for your pet. Of course, there's the standard issue sign of the fish we slap on our bumper that tells the world we love Jesus. All that stuff is great. If we must have something printed on our t-shirt, it might as well be Jesus. You certainly leave the store convinced that Jesus has a huge fan base.

In his recent book, "Not A Fan," pastor Kyle Idleman poses the question: Are you a FAN or FOLLOWER of Jesus? Idleman challenges his readers not to make Jesus simply the object of our admiration, but the very center of our life. Do we seek to be close enough to Jesus to get all the benefits, but not too close that it requires sacrifice?

Fact is, Jesus never chased after people. He employed no public relations firm. Jesus was never interested in our admiration - He wanted our hearts.

Got me to thinking ….. being a true follower of Jesus is all about completely selling out. It is not about giving Jesus some and keeping some for ourselves. Unlike Jesus, we want the admiration of the world as it admires our faith and sacrificial service. The reality of true discipleship comes with a cost.

When you truly follow Jesus you will run against the wind of the world. The scorn of the world will visit your doorstep. Following Jesus may involve sacrificing for others who offer little or no appreciation. Jesus modeled that on the cross.

The most precious blessing of full sellout obedience is the assurance that Jesus is always with us. He doesn't desire or need a fan. He wants a fully committed, fully trusting disciple who will go anywhere at any time He calls.

Football season is upon us - want to be a fan? Buy yourself a jersey. They probably have them at the Christian bookstore.

Missional Is A Word

There's a word widely used in faith circles these days, "missional". It might not be in your dictionary. Even Microsoft Word does not recognize it, keeps popping up on spell check. The word is defined as relating to or connected with a religious mission. Therefore, you and I are missional when we intentionally pursue God's mission for His glory among others. Sounds simple enough - I like the word.

John declared every Christian missional. "The church is sent into the world to continue that which He came to do, in the power of the same Spirit, reconciling people to God." Jesus said, "As the Father has sent Me, I am sending you" (John 20:21).

Got me to thinking ….. this missional thing really broadens the playing field. You don't have to be called away to a foreign land, IE: a full time missionary, to be missional. Spending time in witness to prisoners, wayward youth or folks in a nursing home in your local community is the same as building a school in Katmandu, Nepal.

We are all called to go .... around the world - around the corner. Gotta believe this missional thing really puts us in some awesome company considering Jesus formed the mold. He was sent by the Father. He in turn sent the disciples who in turn carried the gospel beyond. They are our missional ancestors.

Mission is more than a link on our church website. It is the true purpose of the church as God's sent people. We are either defined by mission or simply putting on our best threads and hanging out together on Sunday morning. I suggest our challenge today is to move from a church with mission to a church driven by missional people. There is a difference.

A friend of mine put it best when he described missional as "becoming by grace what Christ is by nature." Man !! ...... I like that. To mirror Jesus in the brokenness of our lives is missional. It is a word. It is our word. Think I'll call Microsoft.

My Generation

Over a million teenagers become pregnant in our nation each year. That equates to one third of all births in America being to parents that are simply children themselves. An expert on family recently spoke of a cycle in our society that runs in a three generation time frame. The first generation is said to GENERATE, the second SPECULATES and the third DISSIPATES. The fourth generation that follows begins the cycle all over again.

 Fond memories abound from the generation of my grandparents. They set an example in the way they lived both in the world as well as their spiritual walk. I have fond memories of my grandmother singing hymns as I worked along beside her in her vegetable garden. I still have the Children's Bible Story book my mom read to me from on a regular basis. The foundation left for my generation set the bar so high that maybe we have laid back and relaxed.

Got me to thinking ….. our grandparents placed the Ten Commandments on the walls of our schools and public buildings just to have their grandchildren lie in our futons of political correctness and and allow them to be removed. The current conditions in our schools are the price paid for that. Our generation must find ways to convey spiritual truth about the goodness and greatness of God to the generation of our children and grandchildren. It is not enough to think or believe it; we must vocalize and live it.

We need to engage them in prayer and participate with them in worship and missional service. Words of encouragement, inspiration and love must be spoken to our children. We must ensure that our witness finds its way into the hearts of the generation we created. We can increase what we have been left or we can squander those blessing thus robbing the generations that follow. Wouldn't it be nice to break the cycle?

"I regret that I didn't spend more time with my children. I accepted too many invitations that produced little meaning in my permanent work."

Rev Billy Graham

Salmon Patties

My wife and I were on NCSU Centennial Campus last week and decided to have lunch at the Farmers Market restaurant. Much to my surprise, salmon patties were the daily special. I had not eaten a salmon patty since I rested my feet under my grandmother's table as a youth.

My most vivid memory of the dish was the disgusting odor that permeated the entire house during and long after preparation. I ordered the salmon patties with fried okra and collards. The collards and okra were great. The patties were not. Truth be known I have never liked salmon patties. It's not about salmon as a food - the Salmon Rheas with lime tomato garlic sauce at Bonefish Grill is to die for. It just seems a waste to grind up the fish and mix it with heaven knows what before frying it up in a cast iron skillet.

The memories I hold around salmon patties are unfounded in the food. The memories are about my grandmother and the things we shared around meal time. She enjoyed cooking for me. It was her kind smile and soft words that I remember most. It was the time she spent with me and the bible stories she read to me from the worn red bound book that sits on my shelf to this day.

It was our trips to the local store where she bought me penny candy and showed me off to all her friends. The salmon patties were just along for the ride.

Salmon patties bring me to reflect on the kind of memories I am creating for my children. The time, or lack thereof, spent with them will shape them into adulthood. Our fast pace world threatens to rob our children of the quality time I shared with my grandparents as a youth. To compensate, we become "Disneyland parents" trying hard to make up ground when all along the only thing our children want from us is our time.

Got me to thinking ….. the world has changed since my childhood. Children are different in their needs and desires but they still need the attention, boundaries and comfort of a Christian home. God commands us to honor our parents. The parents and grandparents in my life left some big shoes for me to fill. Maybe it's time for some salmon - see you at Bonefish Grill.

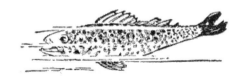

I Do

I thank God every day for my family. I celebrate my marriage. My wife might pen this different but I'd love her just the same. I know of many marriages that are in trouble, way too many. It breaks my heart. I have been through a divorce and I can say it was the most stressful time of my life.

Sometimes I think we approach the challenges of marriage from the wrong angle. There are so many worldly solutions that I think, quite frankly, are just unreasonable. Just scan the magazine rack the next time you are in the grocery checkout line. Read the covers of today's self help magazines. "25 ways to put the fire back in your marriage." If you take the time to read this stuff - there is one thing that is missing - Jesus.

My family attends church and Sunday school every Sunday. There is not even a slight thought of doing otherwise. Will that in itself keep us together? I do know that seeing my wife and son sing in the choir, ring the hand bells and watching my son serve with the adult ushers is a blessing for me that the world cannot match. Sharing our faith does more to cement our marriage bond than hundreds of "date nights", mutual hobbies or candlelight dinners. Knowing that our lives are connected by someone bigger and more powerful provides a sense of security and comfort that goes beyond what we are able to do or say ourselves.

Got to me to thinking ..... about what a dear friend of mine, with tears of pride streaming down his cheeks, shared with me recently. In a group of men he said and I paraphrase - " you have never felt closer to your wife than when you hear her mention your name in her prayers."

That is 100% Jesus stuff. All you marriage self help gurus might what to read HIS book.

Behind The Wall

You leave behind all remnants of the natural world and enter a controlled, artificial one of concrete walls, barbed wire, sliding steel gates and one inch thick glass. You empty your pockets and provide three forms of identification including your Dept of Correction PIN number. It is Job Training Expo day at the Wake County Detention Annex, a political correct name for prison.

Today, instead of lifting weights, watching soap operas or completing correspondence courses, the inmates will be informed of training and job opportunities available to them upon their release. Most are wide eyed and eager to engage. The majority do not deny their involvement in crime. Instead they speak with regret and even remorse. They are eager for a fresh start. A majority will see prison walls again within three years.

These events are usually uplifting and provide you with the "atta boy" that you have done good. More than anything, this time leaves me with a reflection of my own sins. While I have avoided crimes that could put me behind bars, my sins are internal. Not ones of child abuse, theft or robbery. I have never felt any temptation towards these sins. Mine are those of discontent, pride and greed.

Got me to thinking ….. we who battle internal sins may think our sins are more dignified than blatant sins committed by the incarcerated. In his Sermon on the Mount, Jesus paints with one brush pride, greed, lust, hatred and murder. Augustine says it best: "the soul lives by avoiding what it dies by desiring."

As Christians we embrace the concept of grace. There are those among us that do bad things. There are those who choose lifestyles different than ours. There are those who worship in a manner contrary to our practices. There are those who take and those who give. The one thing for certain is that we all fall short of God's expectations.

Sometimes we need to be reminded that the gift of grace is ours - to receive and to give.

Man Up

Someone once told me, or should I say warned me, that getting involved with men's ministry in a leadership role is the toughest thing a man can do. I did not heed the warning. The advice was spot on.

Here are a few observations. First, there is a fraternity forming in the church. A fraternity of men who are being transformed by God's grace. These men are assertive but controlled. They are tough minded yet tender hearted. They are CEOs, construction workers, bankers, unemployed, law enforcement officers, saints and sinners.

What these men have in common is re-prioritization. They have committed to give more time to Jesus. This time is being redirected to small group participation, church attendance, missionary involvement and family. This time is focused on a "full court press" attempt to be Holy - to be like Jesus.

Some things are difficult for men. Forgiving others, not holding grudges or seeking revenge, loving your enemy to name a few. I'm blessed to know men who are making an effort. I often spend time in the closing scriptures of The Old Testament. These passages open the story of Jesus and close with a description of the forming of a new breed of man. "See, I will send you the prophet Elijah before that great and dreadful day of the Lord comes. He will turn the hearts of the fathers to their children, and the hearts of the children to their fathers" (Malachi 4:5-6).

How much clearer does God need to be in what He intends as our future. As with many things in life, there is irony here.

Got me to thinking ….. the true benefactors in a world of transformed men are the women and children. A Holy man is a more faithful husband. A man that resembles Jesus is a more committed father. A man that puts Jesus first in his life is a better role model of what God expects our leadership role to be in the home, at work and in His church.

If you're a man - get on board ……. if you're a woman, pray that he does.

Family Circle

I am haunted by a recent statistic that only 4% of today's youth profess Jesus as their Lord and Savior. There was no television set in the home of Romey and Lucille Gray. There was no mall or movie theater. Their life revolved around three basic elements; Work, Family and Church. They were in church every Sunday, every Sunday night and every Wednesday night. Assuming 2 hours per session (they were Baptist) and 50 weeks out of 52 per year - that is 300 hours per year.

This does not account for the fellowship shared in other activities such as revivals, cleaning the church, meetings, bible studies etc. The small congregation at Smith New Home Baptist Church in Deep Run N.C. was their spiritual and social oasis from the grind of life as tenant farmers in the early and mid 1900s.

The Barna research group estimates the average core member of a church today attends once a week for two hours on average for thirty five weeks per year. This yields seventy hours of spiritual development gatherings. You do the math - that's a 77 percent drop in time spent intentionally developing our spiritual lives.

Got me to thinking ….. imagine a 77% decrease in daily caloric intake, we would suffer from malnutrition if not starvation. A 77% drop in per capita income would bankrupt most of us.

The story goes that when my dad and uncles played school sports, the junior varsity played on Wednesday nights. My grandparents allowed the boys to play, but they chose to attend Wednesday night worship service rather than the sports event. They were making a value statement: there is a place for youth sports, but spiritual community is profoundly more central to life. Lucille would not have been very popular with today's soccer moms.

We all know that fruit doesn't fall far from the tree. You can live your life exemplifying faith, obedience, and integrity. Those who watch and respect you will follow in your footsteps. Worship God together as a family. The return on investment is ever lasting.

Aunt Louisa

They fill their jar and walk the hours back so their children will have water. And then they do it the next day. And they do it the next day. And they do it the next day. There is this maternal impulse, this ancient nurturing instinct and it transcends time. It transcends culture, it transcends economics. There is an ancient mothering impulse - it is a DIVINE impulse.

Take note in Isaiah 66:13. He was speaking to his people who were wondering if they had a future. They were disillusioned and filled with despair. They had very little hope. Of all the images He could have used - He says to them, "Have you ever seen a mother comfort a child? Well this is what God is like. And that is what God is going to do for you."

We all are born with a role. Some of us play that role well - some fail. Last week my aunt Louisa passed. She was not some highly regarded "I am women" in the worldly sense. She was well educated spending her years as a librarian at NC State University. She was a kind, caring and loving lady with a beautiful smile. Her most devoted role was that of a loving mother.

Got me to thinking ….. of the many sacrifices she made so that her only child could excel in life. Financial sacrifices were part of her nature - no niceties for herself - the situation at hand did not allow such. Unselfishness - putting others first - doing without so others could have. This is what pleases God. She believed in the potential of her child and it was that inherent drive which empowered her to tote the jar - day in - day out.

Her son, my cousin, is a success. He gave his mother two grandchildren and one great grandchild. He is a pillar in his community, well respected in his field and active in the leadership of his church. He is a loving father, committed husband and a decent man.

I know that my aunt Louisa has seen the face of God and my faith assures me that she has heard the words "job well done my faithful servant."

You Are Rich

Recently a group from my church attended a fund raiser for ZOE (Zimbabwe Orphan Endeavor). This ministry headed by Rev Greg Jenks focuses on providing assistance to those left orphaned by the AIDS epidemic in Africa. The statistics are overwhelming, the need is great. Every 14 seconds a child is orphaned by this terrible disease. The amount of money I spend each week on coffee would feed a family of three for an entire month. In the world of these orphans, I am a very wealthy man.

One of the most challenging stories in the Bible for me is the encounter between Jesus and a man of wealth. After Jesus had spoken about qualifications to enter the kingdom, the wealthy man asks Jesus what he needs to do. Jesus tells him he lacks one thing.

"Lacks" is a challenging word for the rich man since he thought he had everything. Then Jesus drops the big one: "Sell everything you have and give it to the poor." The man's face sinks and he walks away with his riches. Jesus did not run after the man. Jesus did not try to negotiate or in any way reduce the requirement. Jesus let him walk away.

Got me to thinking ….. in our culture of "seeker sensitivity" and "radical inclusivity", the great temptation is to compromise the cost of discipleship in order to draw a big crowd. Come on in brother, we'll work with you on the cost. We hate to see anyone walk so we clip the claws of the lion, dull the edge of the blade and wipe the blood from the cross.

We pray to God to feed the hungry when our own barns are overflowing. I don't believe Jesus intends to exclude us in our wealth. Rick Warren says it best: "It's not a sin to be rich - It's a sin to die rich."

By the way, regardless of your net worth, if you have a roof over your head, you are rich. If you own a car or have any money in your pocket, you are rich. And finally if you have eaten today and drank clean water, you are rich. In the eyes of the world, you are wealthy - heed the warning. God don't need our money — He wants our obedience. Don't worry - when He becomes the center of our lives — we lack nothing.

Mother's Day

Today is my birthday - happy birthday to me. To make matters worse, it is the big black fifty. Got my AARP card in the mail recently. As we get older the anniversary of our birth takes on a different meaning. The way we celebrate this event is shaped by events in our lives.

Since leaving home in 1976 for college, my mother always called me on my birthday. The call always came around 8:00AM. Particularly in my younger years, some mornings I was sleeping in after a late night and really did not feel like talking. Other mornings I was already celebrating. But always by the end of our chat I was glad she called.

Got me to thinking ….. she NEVER missed a single year. She always assured me how much she loved me and how my birthday was a very special day for her. Of course she would also use this time to make me feel guilty about not visiting enough and would always end our conversation with " I love You Son. " This continued until 1995 the year she passed away. Since then, as birthdays come and go, I miss that phone call.

Since that time, June 29th has become more of a celebration of my mother and the unconditional love she had for me. It was not until I lost that phone call that I fully appreciated her love, concern, closeness and unselfishness.

My mother was a devoted Christian lady. She had, long before her death, prayed the sinner's prayer and lived her life serving God in all she did. She was kind and giving. She always had a smile and something positive to say regardless of the circumstances. She set a Godly example for my sister and me and had us in church on Sunday whether we wanted to go or not. Very simply put - she was a wonderful lady and an awesome mother.

Each year on my birthday, around 8:00 AM she is with me. My faith provides me that celebration. On my birthday each year I do not celebrate another year of myself. I celebrate that my mother now lies in the arms of Jesus awaiting my arrival.

Don't Look Back

When I was younger I was addicted to running. Throughout high school, college and even into my early and mid thirties, I ran every single day. I enjoyed running but not competitively. Whenever I ran competitively I became obsessed with looking over my shoulder. That is a no-no. It slows you down. It breaks your stride. It wrecks your rhythm. Many times we refer to life as a race, most often a "rat" race.

I have come to realize, if we want to run the race of life successfully, we can't look back. Paul, along the same lines, suggests in Philippians 3:13, "Forgetting those things which are behind looking forward to what is ahead." Here, the word "forget" doesn't mean a failure to remember as much as it means no longer being influenced or affected by the past.

While you may not be able erase things from your memory, you don't need to let them influence you. Sometimes we dredge up the things God has forgiven and forgotten. In Jeremiah 31:34 the Lord says, "I will remember their sins no more." Yet many times we will bring up past sins, forgetting the fact that our God has a bigger eraser.

Got me to thinking ….. if God has forgiven our sins, then we need to leave them behind, learn from our mistakes, not do the same thing again, and move forward. Why should we choose to remember what God has chosen to forget? He has given us, through the gift of grace, a wonderful opportunity to make a fresh start and establish a permanent, personal relationship with Him.

This race of life we all are running can be tough. Unemployment, sickness, financial pressures, broken families, challenged relationships test our fitness and spiritual conditioning. It's like a marathon in 98 degree heat with feet pounding the pavement and muscles burning with the finish line nowhere in sight.

To that I can only say - keep running brothers and sisters. The good news is that God is with us. No need to look back.

Under The Influence

Those who visit my office rarely leave without commenting on the 8X12 framed photo of yours truly with Diane Sawyer. This 8X12 hangs beside the 5X7 of my wife. Say What !!!! Folks usually say something like "is that who I think it is?" Well we all know she is a lovely lady and it was quite a delight for me and my family to meet her a few years back.

Her beauty recently graced the cover of Parade magazine. The focus of the article was how Diane, now a prime time news anchor, wields power in her celebrity. It appears that Diane is using hers for good causes. The article was titled "I Want To Be A Powerful Witness."

I suggest the three things we all have to offer are time, money and influence. We all have influence. While our realm of persuasion may not match that of a prime time news anchor, we all have influence.

Diane talks about turning pain into purpose. She talks about how she used her influence to help orphans inspired by a sermon she once heard. She recognizes that she can make a larger impact on good by influencing others compared to what she might do alone. The fact that she remains grounded and loyal to the teachings of life is a breath of fresh air in today's world of dysfunctional celebrity.

Got me to thinking ….. about the powerful witness and the results of Diane Sawyer doing good in the world. This is what God expects of her and what He expects from each of us. We all have influence and we also have the choice of how we use it.

As for the 8x12 of Diane versus the 5X7 of my wife. I'm safe, the 8x12 was a gift from the 5x7. Now that's influence.

Infamous

Read something in a book last week that kinda rubbed me the wrong way. John Lennon, in an interview during the height of the Beatles fame, complained about having to sing " I want to hold your hand" for the rest of his life. Guess what Johnnie boy ..... the song made you rich and famous. Same kinda thing hearing how Pete Rose flies into a rage of anger whenever a fan approaches him for an autograph. Hello Pete - it's the fans that bought the tickets that bought you all your toys my friend.

There are many other examples ..... Michael Jackson and Elvis to name a couple that simply did not find happiness in fame and fortune. Lennon and Rose spent years of practice and sacrifice to reach the level of professional status only to gripe and complain once they got there.

Got me to thinking ..... what is really important? Makes you wonder what we really hold close. What are the things we should be thankful for? I will suggest the greatest blessings are family, friends and our relationship with Jesus. All other things are of the world and somehow seem to be unfulfilling once we get them.

We are warned about storing up treasures of the world. They are manmade, artificial and carry a shelf life equal only to the length of our fascination with them. Our recent economic downturn has provided evidence of just how quickly our worldly gods can vaporize.

On this day, and every day, I am thankful for Jesus, His church and His Holy Spirit. Our Lord is the same today as He was yesterday and will be tomorrow. His precious love for each of us does not fluctuate with Wall Street, fortune or fame.

Old Things Made New

If you visit my home you may see several old things that appear new. There is the 1950 Farmall Tractor, the 1962 John Deere 110 and the 1976 Vann wood splitter to name a few. They all are old but appear new because they have been restored. These are items from my past that provide fond memories.

These memories and "things" are mostly wrapped around the time shared with my dad. Because I cherish these things I have restored them. They all were once worn, torn and broken. Because of my love for them and the memories they hold, I have committed a significant amount of time and work on them. Now they appear brand new.

People also, at times in their lives, need restoration. The pain and suffering brought on by the world breaks us down, wears on us and at times steals from us our hope. Just like the items I mentioned above, people need time and help from others to bring restoration to their lives. Rather than judging, finding fault or gossiping about others when they hurt - we should engage them in a positive way.

We should re-paint them with our time. We should repair their cracked edges and brokenness with our love. We should straighten the bent parts with our presence and support. We should replenish their hope with our prayers.

Got me to thinking ..... suffering and being in a spiritual funk can be a lonely place. Our hope gauge registers empty. We doubt ourselves and sometimes even question God. These are times when our faith rubber really needs to meet the road of renewal. It is in this place that we need each other.

There is no greater service or responsibility as a Christian than to play a role in the restoration of a brother or sister. We hear in Psalm 51:12 "restore to me the joy of your salvation and grant me a willing spirit to sustain me." The process creates a very special bond that is everlasting. It is what God expects.

No Where To Run

It was a treat for me as a child to visit my uncle Buck and aunt Lucy. They lived on a farm in Cove City, a rural community located between Kinston and New Bern. Now when I say rural, I'm talking about mile after mile of flat farmland and massive stands of timber. One of the highlights of those visits was the chance that I might see a deer. Often at dusk, if you were lucky, you might sight one far off in a field of soybeans or at the tree line. This was an awesome treat for me as a child.

Today, I see as many as ten deer in my backyard daily. They eat all my vegetation and seem as comfortable and domesticated as my pet dogs. The road leading to my subdivision is frequently littered with the carcasses of those who were no match for the overcrowded roadway. This is a sad state of affairs. What are we doing to God's creation? When will we have enough drug stores and Chinese take outs?

Got me to thinking ….. about Genesis 1:26. God commands that we be good stewards of his creation.

It is puzzling to me that people who claim to take God's word seriously fail to act urgently to stop the rapid molestation of what was first created as a beautiful and peaceful garden.

God's instructions for the people of Israel to let farmland rest every seventh year allowed for the conservation of good, productive land. When are we as a people going to be satisfied with what we have? When are we going to let our natural resources rest and be satisfied in our current balance with nature? When will the lust for more and better end? When will we learn to share His space with God's creatures?

The sighting of these beautiful animals no longer brings the joy for me as it did as a child. All the fish in the sea, the birds in the sky and the animals that scurry along the ground are our responsibility. I wonder if God is happy with the job we are doing.

The Immigrant

I was born in a foreign land. My family was middle class. My father ran a pharmacy. Being middle class in my country was dangerous. Only the very rich and very poor are safe. The poor are protected and used as pawns by the rich to secure aid from wealthy countries like the US. When the aid arrives it is captured by the rich and never reaches the poor.

Throughout my childhood I feared for my life. My parents would keep me in closets so I would not be detected when the government searched our home. I once spent 3 months in a closet without seeing sunlight. I was a mama's boy. I did not get outside. I mostly stayed inside and helped her inside the home.

When I was seventeen my parents made the decision for me to leave home. I walked barefoot for 21 days to Sudan. 10 of those days were without food. I was forced to constantly hide in the tall grass for protection. I have been shot at, robbed, beaten, stalked and chased like an animal. I've slept in graveyards, lived in the filth of refugee camps and eaten bug infested handouts from soup kitchens.

The toughest part was going years without any contact with my mother. The government killed my father. They ran him over with a car then riddled his body with bullets for good measure. My older brother was also murdered along with many cousins and relatives. I am sure I would have met the same fate if my parents had not forced me to flee.

I did not come to your country for economic gain. I came to save my life. The US is now my country. God has been in my life since age seven. He has been with me in my journey. All the suffering I have experienced has been His will. He has blessed me with a wife, three children and a home in the United States - all glory be to Him.

As told to my men's group by an immigrant friend. Got me to thinking ….. what do you have to be thankful for today ?

The Furry Physician

Several years ago my wife and I spent quite a bit of time at the hospital. Our son, twelve years old at the time, was ill and one of us was by his bedside round the clock. A hospital is a stressful place especially the children's area. There is constant crying, doors slamming, IV dispenser alarms buzzing - you know - sounds of illness and distress.

With this being said, all was not bad. There were the visits from the doggies. Wake Med has a wonderful program that allows pets and their owners to visit children while hospitalized. My family can attest, this is a great program. The highlight of Joseph's day was the visits from his newfound furry friends. The owners were nice as well. What an awesome ministry in bringing happiness into an otherwise stale and bland environment.

Got me to thinking ..... who can deny that God created animals, or that His eye is on each and every sparrow and German Sheppard that He has made (Matthew 10:29-31.) Studies conducted by James Bossard, a children's socialization expert, reveal that pets give confidence to children who lack it, security to children who are afraid and emotional support to many who could not otherwise enjoy life. Research also has shown that animals know more than most of us suppose and often have an uncanny sensitivity to the thoughts and feelings of people.

This was a very taxing time for our family. Our son spent nearly a month in the hospital. Our entire rhythm of life was turned upside down. During that time the only thing that mattered was getting him well and back home. There was something very sacred about those doggie visits. Those furry friends were indeed instruments through which the hope and love of God were experienced. Isaiah 11:6 ensures that animals will have a place in the kingdom of God - for that I give thanks.

Earl The Pearl

I hate what happened to Tiger Woods, Mark McGuire, Kobe Bryant and the rest of the fallen millionaire athletes. I know they are human and the wealth and celebrity they enjoy brings about a level of temptation that I will never experience and that's probably a good thing. My heart and prayers go out to these guys but they owe me nothing. They were not my role models. They were not men I looked up to or strived to in any way pattern my life by.

I do have role models. There is my dad and father-n-law who are both saints in my book. Both these guys have figured it out and are dedicated to the true things that are important in life. I will never be like these men but my admiration and desire to be like them really keeps me on my toes ..... gives me something to chase.

I will add another to this list, my uncle Earl. He, like my dad, is now with Jesus. He was my dad's younger brother and his best friend. I loved to hear the stories he told of him and my dad checking their rabbit boxes each day after school. The friendship they shared was solid.

I loved him because he loved my dad so deeply. Uncle Earl loved his Lord. He was a true disciple that understood what it took to reach others. He knew that living his life in a Christ like manner was far more effective than sticking his finger in your face. He took that responsibility seriously. He challenged you with a cutting edge but encouraged you with enthusiasm. He led with a firmness wrapped in humility.

Got me to thinking ….. Uncle Earl never had a triple double on the basketball court, was not a home run king nor did he ever win the Masters. What he did was live his life in a way that inspired others. His life was living proof that happiness and respect can be obtained within the borders of decency, kindness and love. He was a faithful husband, firm but loving father, leader in his church and a friend that could be counted on regardless of the situation.

When we meet again and we will, I can only hope he is proud of me for attempting to follow his lead.

Radical Generosity

It is that time of year when we focus on giving. The folks that peddle gift wrap do very well in December. Retailers are running ads, offering coupons and opening early to promote drastic price mark downs. These tactics do work. They create shopping frenzies. Sad to realize that several people were actually killed recently in stampedes created by such promotions.

When it comes to charities, it is a widely held perception that corporations and foundations are the largest givers when in fact individuals comprise 82.4% of total charitable giving according to recent statistics. Enough with the statistics.

Got me to thinking ….. about the parables Jesus used in His teachings that addressed giving. These teachings suggest we give all we can every day. We are encouraged to give regardless of our wealth, ability or stature. Gifts are simple acts freely given and freely received. We have no excuse to neglect those in need. It is easy to hand over this responsibility to the church or government but Jesus demands our personal involvement in giving to those in need.

I have come to realize that the greatest gifts are not purchased at the mall or wrapped and tied with a bow. The most precious gifts lie at the tips of our fingers when we extend a hand to those in need. No gift is greater than a smile or a minute of your time given to another who needs a listener.

These personal gifts of love and understanding are provided to us by Gods spirit with the hope we pass them along. So may we answer the call of God to give and in return receive the blessing of helping others? I can testify that the rewards are far greater than a tax deduction.

Everyone regardless of income, available time, age or skills can do something useful for others and in the process strengthen the fabric of our shared humanity.

President Bill Clinton

Prudent Stewardship

My first job out of college in 1981 was with Wachovia Bank. At that time it was a solid organization founded and operated under sound business principles. Our CEO was John G. Medlin. Mr. Medlin was voted by his peers as the top CEO in the county numerous times. At lunch he could often be found in line at KFC with coupon in hand after driving there in his 15 year old Plymouth sedan. He cared little about the Wall Street image.

Now the bank is busted. Single mom employees have been kicked to the curb with the $500 wingtip slippers of current management. Today's financial crisis bears little resemblance to the economic collapse of the late 1920s. Capitalism is not in crisis. The fundamentals of the American economy remain strong. American innovation, a dedicated labor force, strong consumer demand, vast natural resources, and unlimited intellectual capital is alive and well. Our current crisis is a product of greed.

Got me to thinking …. The desire for a profit and material gain is not in itself greed. The Bible clearly teaches that the worker is worthy of his hire and that rewards should follow labor, thrift, and investment. However - given the nature of this fallen world and the reality of human sinfulness, greed is a constant temptation.

Christians should commit to Christ like participation in our economy. False valuations are not optimistic opinions, they are lies. Insider trading is not strategic information gathering, it's a form of theft. Today's crisis in the financial system need not be a threat to the long-term health and vitality of our economic system.

Let us be reminded that everything we are, everything we do, and everything we own truly belongs to God. It is to be available for Kingdom purposes. This world is not our home and our treasure is not found here. Here's an investment tip for you. We are to do all, invest all, own all, purchase all to the glory of God.

The return is eternal.

Joy Of Toys

As a youngster my birthday was the only time of year except Christmas that I received toys. There were no weekly trips to the mall, eBay, craigslist or on-line shopping. The excitement and joy in my birthday celebrations was measured by the content of boxes wrapped up around the birthday cake. This pattern continued into adulthood. Heck, I have often used my birthday as an excuse to buy adult toys for myself.

My birthday was last week and I didn't get a single toy. It was a great day however. The first gift I received was a message from ZOE Ministries calling to confirm the safe arrival of my wife and son in Africa. That was a great gift knowing they were in a foreign country serving those less fortunate.

As the day progressed, I received phone calls and e-mails conveying birthday wishes. There were some very special conversations with Christian brothers and sisters who provide spiritual gifts for me year round.

Got me to thinking ….. there are several accounts in Mark, Luke and Matthew when Jesus speaks of selling all we have and giving to the poor and needy. Many folks, including myself have struggled with that concept. We are more accustomed to buying than selling. Sometimes there is huge guilt and confusion when we enjoy our consumer driven lifestyles of plenty and abundance. It is not an easy thing to let go of our toys.

I recognized, more than ever this birthday that toys cannot fill the void in our hearts the way God can. When we are empty there is no material object money can buy that can fill our hearts and minds with peace the way Jesus can. Jesus has no problem with our toys until they become the center of our lives.

Because the love that God has for us is complete in every way, it's the ultimate birthday gift that lasts a lifetime .... an eternal lifetime.

Dr Ted

I had the opportunity recently to spend some time along the restored waterfront area of downtown Wilmington. Although the weather was great outside, I spent most of my day in the hospital. Now wait ... don't be alarmed, I was not ill. I was there visiting friends that are launching a ministry they call "Mission Ready" to recycle medical supplies and equipment.

Millions of dollars in medical supplies and equipment are discarded by hospitals across American each year. Syringes, gloves, lab and clinical supplies, still in their original packaging are tossed. I saw over one million dollars worth of used, but good as new, anesthesia and x-ray machines sitting in the basement corner of a hospital. One person's trash is another person's treasure, or so the saying goes. In this case we are talking about people's lives.

Got me to thinking ..... how our trash can be an answer to prayer for the staff at a needy medical center in an underdeveloped country. My coastal friends are determined to make a difference. These are people like my friend Dr. Ted. He is a highly trained trauma physician who has offered his time and skills for years to the needy in Africa and most recently Haiti. He has seen mothers die because there were no simple tools to close the wound from a routine c-section birth procedure. Ted's passion to serve is fueled by his knowing that infants are dying of infection from rusty razors being used to cut their umbilical cord. Life saving solutions to these stories sit in our trash cans back home. While our brothers and sisters are dying, we are filling our landfills.

Our weekend cumulated Saturday evening with a concert to benefit our efforts. National recording artist Sister Hazel together with the Wilmington Symphony Orchestra entertained a sold out crowd at Kenan Auditorium. The band got their name from an African American lady who ran a rescue mission in their hometown of Gainesville Florida.

This sister, named Hazel, inspired the band with her unconditional concern for all beings in need. She would have been right at home with us this weekend. Through the commitment and dedication of my "Mission Ready" friends ...... help is on the way !!!

Her Life Is Fantastic

Coffins should come in only one size. Built full size to accommodate an adult body. They should not be child size. Just doesn't seem right. Last week I attended the funeral services for an eight year old young lady in our community. Her name was Madison. I understand she was a smart student, generous and caring. She was a cheerleader and lover of animals.

I did not know Madison or her family personally. They needed a large church for the service so we provided our facility. Having children of my own I felt lead to attend. There were kind words spoken by Madison's grandmother and two of her teachers. It seems that this young lady was a very special person. I could not help wondering what she could have become, what contributions she might have made to our world and the people around her.

Got me to thinking ….. of all the things said by the preachers, teachers and grandmother - something said by Madison soothed and blessed me the most. In a recent entry in her dairy she simply wrote: "My life is fantastic." Those four words speak volumes for her life - the kind of parents she had - the environment in which she was growing into a young lady.

The death of a child shakes us into the awareness that life is very short. It reminds us that life is on loan from God. We do well to understand as much as we can its length and breadth. The good news is as Christians we know that death will not have the final say over Madison. She is now leading an even more fantastic life with Jesus, a life eternal.

But Jesus called them to him, saying,
"Let the children come to
me, and do not hinder them,
for to such belongs the kingdom of God."

Luke 18:16

Time

I spent some time this week sending notes to folks with numbers attached to their name. John Doe #0998745. Athletes have numbers. We know Michael Jordan as number 23, Dale Earnhardt as number 3. In many cases, the number is more recognizable than the person. The numbers associated with my friends this week were North Carolina Department of Correction numbers. These numbers you need to make it through life without.

I have been involved with a prison ministry for several years working with inmates in their reentry process. For many, the outside is more challenging than the inside. Where do they go, live or work? This is a critical time and depending on what happens usually determines if they make it on the outside or if they reenter prison. Over 700,000 inmates are released each year. Well over half will return to prison within three years.

I have a file cabinet full of letters from inmates. Some letters are testimonies of rehabilitation and rebirth while others are filled with excuses and hateful blame. The overwhelming theme that flows throughout these correspondences is the concept of time. Many letters begin with "I will be released soon" only to find in the following paragraph their release date is five years down the calendar. Time is elusive and mysterious in the world that is a 64 square feet enclosure.

Got me to thinking ….. while we on the outside use time as a measure to sequence events, compare intervals and quantify change - there is no need of such for those whose lives are absent of any elements other than a bed, sink and toilet. Ironically, you will never see a prison cell without a calendar pinned to the wall.

Jesus knew about time. He knew from the beginning how little of it He possessed. He knew with each passing day what awaited Him in the end. Time was not on His side. Jesus wasted no time. He was quick to surround himself with a group similar to the kinds of folk He was trying to reach. He was quick to teach, educate and delegate within His inner circle. In doing so, He also taught us not to worry about time. Much was accomplished in the three short years of His ministry.

How much time do you have?

Blame Me

With spring time here, I dropped my motorcycle off at the dealer for a service check-up. I am very particular about the mechanical condition of my motorcycle. Thoughts of mechanical failure at 70 mph on two wheels cultivate images of blunt force trauma.

Anyway, there on the wall of the service department was a sign: "NOT RESPONSIBLE FOR YOUR MOTORCYCLE." Uhmmmmmm ...... now if the dealer is not responsible for my motorcycle while it is in their possession then who is ????   Got me to thinking ..... about responsibility.

We live in a world where everything we do, write, say and even think is wrapped around liability. Who is liable? Who is responsible? It's enough to make you want to crawl in a hole and hide. Is McDonalds really to blame when you spill a cup of hot coffee in your lap while driving and texting? We all know the drill.

Coming out the other side of my thought process I realized that claiming responsibility is an awesome opportunity for our church. Being responsible is being compassionate. Being responsible is being supportive. Being responsible and being intentional in the process is an awesome witness to all those around us.

As Christians we are called to be responsible to and for each other and to God. The poor, the naked and the hungry are all the responsibility of each of us. Provision for others is a fundamental responsibility of what we ought to be as Christians. When the world sees the church being responsible - powerful things happen. Witness occurs.

I recently read this quote - "Voodoo has been in my family, but the government isn't helping us. The only people giving aid are the Christian churches." This comes from a 24 year old Port-au-Prince resident who joined a Christian church days after the Haiti earthquake.

There will come a day when we will certainly be held accountable for our acts of responsibility .... for God has entrusted each of us with ourselves.

Goodbye ... my friend

I played God last week. It was very painful. For me - the stakes were high. The commodity was precious. The decision affected loved ones. I have never trusted a man who didn't love a dog. I love dogs. I have had many over the years. Loved em all - some were special. Biggie, my English bulldog was special.

My family acquired him through a divorce settlement. His owners at the time operated the kennel that boarded our pets when we vacationed. Their marriage was ending and they chose us as their first choice to adopt this handsome young man.

From the very beginning we were joined at the hip. We did everything together except ride the Harley .... and I was working on that. Whenever I was at home he was my shadow. He loved to go to work with me and relax all day under my desk. He loved me unconditionally and I returned my affection likewise.

Whenever he would barge in the house and rub on the furniture I would always come to his defense. Biggie and I spent quality "man" time together in a way that only dog lovers could appreciate.

Several months ago my friend became ill. After some testing it was determined he had probably had a heart attack. He had been a weekly patient at the NCSU Vet School for some time having fluid drawn from his body. At first, it seemed to be working even though the doctors that supervised his care were honest with us. We were told that his condition would probably deteriorate and it did.

Last week I made the decision for my dear friend's suffering to come to an end. His quality of life was reduced to recurring seizures and loss of half of his body weight. Once a robust 78 pound beautiful and energetic friend had been reduced to constant suffering.

God has given man domain over the animals. To me Biggie was not an animal - he was my friend. We communicated and clearly had a relationship that was special to each of us. Last week I did not play God. Last week I dug deeper than I thought I ever could and found the God given compassion in my heart to make an unselfish decision to help a friend.

Affirmations

* Very well written. I felt your passion and emotion. Where do you get all this stuff? Keep on Brother.

* I would appreciate your permission to use a part of your story as a bulletin insert on Sunday. It will tie in well with my sermon on Radical discipleship. Thanks Charlie for these jewels.

* Brother you have been a witness to more people than you will ever know, and have caused a lot of men to be strengthened in their own faith.

* Your devotions inspire and challenge me. Thanks for sharing and continuing to be open to God's calling for your life.

* Charlie - I absolutely love your devotionals and really look forward to what you're going to say next. You have a gift. Please keep these coming so that I start my week off right.

* This is wonderful! Love how you write what is on your heart. It's like an actual conversation. Have you considered putting these in a book or on a blog.

* Phenomenal message. I keep thinking that I know it, have heard it, etc. Your devotional fires me up for the day! I am paralyzed, but I feel like I can go ten rounds with Lennox Lewis. Keep them coming.

* Charlie: I needed this message today. You always come through. Thanks so much and hope your week is as you like it!

* I needed this today. God Bless you Charlie Gray!

* Your devotions are so well spoken. This is what I love about you, it is honest and forthright and hits the nail on the head. What more could you ask for in a Christian brother. Thanks

* Thanks for another awesome and timely message. I send these to my friends and they love them also.

* Thanks for including me in your messages each week. I look forward to reading them and passing them along to some of my friends. Thanks again for your weekly inspirations.

* Charlie, I admire your commitment to this work.

* You must be inundated with comments about your devotions, but I must say how very impressed I am with your insightful perspective and your gift of eloquently yet concisely communicating it to a vast audience... Thanks for sharing!

* Charlie, thanks for sending these devotionals every week. I look forward to reading them and starting my week out on the right foot. I am very impressed with your insight and wisdom! Have you considered putting these in a book?

* For awhile now I have been studying scripture with a good friend of mine via chat in the evenings. He attends a messianic congregation. At any rate, the more I learn and understand the true meaning of scripture, the more your devotionals make sense.

* This is going on my bulletin board. Thanks, Charlie!

* Dearest Charlie, I loved these. You have no idea how much they make me smile. Thanks for sharing!

* What a wonderful message Charlie. I continue to be amazed at your consistency and endurance with your Monday morning devotionals. I am also envious of your writing skills. I would wager that there is many a published author who would put down their own pens to be able to write with yours.

* I have been neglectful in telling you how much I have begun to look forward to your weekly devotion. You are a gifted writer and express ideas and concepts with clarity and genuine love of the Word. I appreciate your gift and that you share it with us.

* Charlie, Please tell our little alien friend that I am proud of him. According to Matthew 5:11 Jesus is too!

* "As you commit to mission and ministry know that God never wastes our pain."

* Thanks for saying what needs to be said and what so many of us need to hear. Keep up the great works!

* Are you sure that you are not called to preach????

* I continue to enjoy what you write .. perhaps you should put these into a devotional book and publish? God is blessing many through your work.

* Hey, I know one thing we have in common. Both our grandparents raised tobacco. I always tell people that's where my Puritan work ethic comes from! Did you ever think you might be called to <u>preach</u>? 'cause I think you can do some preachin'!

* This is a very important warning message for me right now in my life. Your message could not be timelier. Thank you for helping me to find the strength to make it through one more day brother.

* You are an awesome torchbearer for our ministry to men. You capture such emotion with your words. May God continue to bless your efforts my friend.

* My brother - thanks for sharing emotions that we all have, whether we like to admit them or not.

* Charlie, Thank you for your devotionals! I think they are really on target. God is calling us to follow thru on our commitments & your words are encouraging us to do just that.

* I continued to be amazed at the way you are able to assemble such clear and concise devotional messages from ordinary daily life – Nicely done!

* I have been neglectful in telling you how much I have begun to look forward to your Sunday night email. You are a gifted writer and express ideas and concepts with clarity and genuine love of the Word. I appreciate your gift and that you share it with me.

* Your words today are an answer to my prayers. God has a way of being there when you need Him.

Made in the USA
Charleston, SC
01 July 2012